Understanding the Blood of Christ

David Alsobrook

Foreword by
Judson Cornwall

Sovereign World

Sovereign World Ltd
PO Box 777
Tonbridge
Kent TN11 9XT
England

First printing of Revised Edition August 1986
Second printing of Revised Edition October 1993
Third printing of Revised Edition June 1995

The original book has been printed in India in the Telugu language
and published partially in Spanish and Cebuano also.

Sure Word Ministries, PO Box 2305, Brentwood, Tennessee 37024

ISBN: 1 85240 166 4

Typeset by CRB Associates, Norwich
Printed in England by Clays Ltd, St Ives plc

Understanding the Blood of Christ supersedes and replaces *The Precious Blood* and *The Precious Blood Study Guide*.

Special Note

Whenever I am referring to the blood of Christ, but have simply said 'the Blood' in order to not be redundant, I have chosen to capitalize the 'b' so the reader will understand it to mean His special blood. When the meaning is clear that it is His blood that is referred to, the 'b' is left uncapitalized throughout the book.

All references to deity are capitalized whether or not that version of the Bible capitalized them.

Contents

Foreword

From the days of Cain through the Charismatic renewal, there have been many persons bent on having a bloodless religion. Just as Cain preferred to offer God the work of his hands, so many persons seek to offer God their gifts, ministries or doctrines as sacrifices. They function as though their own righteousness or spirituality were redemptive for their lives. They do not want to be dependent on the work of another, but true redemption is exclusively through the blood of Jesus.

While we New Testament Christians have been spared the messy ritual of slaughtering animals and sprinkling their blood upon the altar and upon the garments of the person making sacrifice, we still need the ministry of the blood on and in our lives. God has not recanted His requirement *'Without the shedding of blood is no remission'* (Hebrews 9:22).

The theme of the entire Bible is 'The Lamb of God'. He is pictured typically in Israel's sacrifices, but He is revealed in the New Testament as Jesus Christ the Son of God. He died that we might live. He bore our sins on Calvary and shed His blood to put away our sins once and for all. The New Testament promises: *'The blood of*

Jesus Christ his Son cleanseth us from all sin' (1 John 1:7).

Today's self-centred generation of Christians needs to look away to Calvary. We need to learn and experience again the protection of the blood, justification by the blood, sanctification by the blood, and restoration by the blood. Without this dynamic work of the blood of Jesus, our pop-psychology sermons may change minds, but they will not change lives. Only the blood of Jesus can transform sinners into saints.

David Alsobrooks's book, *Understanding the Blood of Christ*, brings us face to face with the powerful blood of Jesus and applies it to modern living. We may not be nomadic shepherds, but we are lost sinners whose only chance of change lies in the power of the precious blood of Jesus. When it is properly applied to the life, drug addicts are released from the power of dope. This blood of Jesus is still releasing persons from the nearly hopeless grip of sensuality and lust, and it is providing healing for broken bodies.

> There's no power like the power of the blood.
> There's no power like the cleansing healing flood.
> No power against it ever stood.
> Hallelu! Hallelu! Hallelu!

Judson Cornwall

Chapter 1

The Precious Blood

The concept of making a sacrifice in the minds of most believers today is to give up something of value, or endure something of hardness for the Lord. This concept is formed in our thinking due to the biblical procedure of sacrificing to God. When Araunah [1] freely offered King David the threshingfloor and the oxen to sacrifice unto the Lord, David replied, *'No, but I will surely buy it from you for a price; nor will I offer burnt offerings to the LORD my God with that which costs me nothing'* (2 Samuel 24:24). **A sacrifice which cost the sacrificer nothing was not a sacrifice**. An ancient Israelite would search out the best of the flock and would pay the owner a suitable price. Then he would bring the animal to the priest to offer it to the Lord.

The most costly sacrifice in the Old Testament was Solomon's offering at the dedication of the Temple. Never before had Israel seen a greater sacrifice in terms of material cost. We are told this in 1 Kings 8:62–64:

> *'Then the king and all Israel with him offered sacrifices before the LORD. And Solomon offered a sacrifice of peace offerings, which he offered to the LORD, twenty-two thousand bulls and one hundred and*

twenty thousand sheep. So the king and all the children of Israel dedicated the house of the LORD. On the same day the king consecrated the middle of the court that was in the front of the house of the LORD; for there he offered burnt offerings, grain offerings, and the fat of the peace offerings, because the bronze altar that was before the LORD was too small to receive the burnt offerings, the grain offerings, and the fat of the peace offerings.'

It is hard to imagine the actual cost of such a huge sacrifice. Their economy, of course, was much smaller than ours and based on the agrarian system of a farming nation. By our standard of measurement it would probably cost more than $13 million to buy these animals on the open market. By their standards this was worth much more than it would be to us today.

The blood of these sacrifices doubtless measured into the tens of thousands of gallons. The blood from three oxen would fill an average bathtub. Twenty-two thousand oxen were offered. One hundred and twenty thousand sheep would make a sea of white in a large field. It staggers the imagination to think how great this offering actually was. It was so large, in fact, that the large Brazen Altar was *'too small to receive'* the offerings. The middle of the court (the entire area where the altar was) became the place of sacrifice. We are not told how many priests were busy at work, or how long it took to offer these sacrifices. One thing is certain: it took hours and hours and was performed by hundreds of priests.

Few of the Israelites had seen as much livestock in their lifetime, let alone at one time. God's ancient people were doing well to sacrifice an occasional lamb. Some were so poor they could hardly afford the nominal cost of pigeons or doves.

This dedicatory sacrifice was never equaled in Israel's history. The modernists of today regard this sacrifice as one huge waste. Even the moderates question, 'Would not a few animals provide the necessary blood requirement?' The Law contained no commandment to offer such a great assemblage of flocks and herds.

While meditating on this passage, the Holy Spirit gave an insight into this unusual event. **Solomon was sacrificing by a revelation!** *He foresaw the inestimable cost of the perfect Lamb God required.* Jesus is God's Lamb. The Father searched out the best of heaven; second-best would not do. Only the Anointed One in His bosom would qualify for the title, *'The Lamb of God.'* Such was not an ordinary lamb, nor an ordinary man. [2] The Word sent from heaven became flesh and dwelt among us and we beheld His glory! (see John 1:14). Solomon's costly sacrifice was but a mite in comparison with the sacrifice sent from God. In keeping with the aforesaid principle that 'a sacrifice is not a sacrifice unless it costs the sacrificer something,' God's Lamb cost Him much. Salvation did not come cheap.

Why His Blood Is Precious

> *'Knowing that you were not redeemed with corruptible things, like silver or gold, from your aimless conduct received by tradition from your fathers, but with the precious blood of Christ, as of a lamb without blemish and without spot.'* (1 Peter 1:18–19)

The blood of Christ is precious. He is endeared to us by His blood and we to Him by the same. One meaning of the word 'precious' is dear, as is often said, 'they are precious people,' etc. To be accurate, 'precious' means 'costly, valuable, honorable, highly esteemed, and beloved'. The 'Precious Blood' therefore means the costly, valuable, honorable, highly esteemed, and beloved Blood.

In verse 18 Peter tells us we **are not redeemed** with corruptible things, and in verse 19 he tells us we **are redeemed** by the blood of Christ. If we are not redeemed with corruptible things and we **are** redeemed by the Blood, then the Blood is incorruptible. [3] In verse 18 the apostle informs that we are not redeemed with silver and gold. These two metals are among the most rare, valuable, and costly metals throughout the world. Gold is precious whereas gravel is common.

The blood of Christ is just as rare, valuable, and precious compared to animal blood as are silver and gold compared to iron and lead. His blood is costly – the best God had to offer. It cost the Father and the Son much to provide salvation for us. **His blood is rare – there is no other blood like it.** His blood is 'highly esteemed' in heaven where the saints often speak and sing about it and their Lamb [4] (see Revelation 5:9; 7:9–14). The blood of Christ is beloved of the Father and beloved of every true born child of God.

Paul admonished the Ephesian elders, '. . . *feed the church of God,* **which He hath purchased with His own blood**' (Acts 20:28). Notice that neither the Name nor Person of Jesus Christ are mentioned in this passage at all. The Second Person of the Godhead has no direct reference. ('He' and 'His' in verse 28 are personal pronouns which refer back to the proper noun 'God.') It is true that *'God is a Spirit'* (John 4:24), and that *'flesh and blood cannot inherit the kingdom of God'* (1 Corinthians 15:50). However, God can make anything and everything. All the blood in Jesus' body *was made by the creation power of the Father*. **For this**

reason Jesus' blood is of a higher type than common blood. We have a better covenant established upon better promises because better Blood ratified it (see Hebrews 8:6). God the Father, through Jesus, purchased the Church with His blood.

Peter tells us we are 'redeemed' by the precious blood of Christ. The Greek word he employed had the meaning of purchasing a slave out of the slave market. Jesus paid the price for our redemption with His **costly Blood alone!** We are purchased from the slavery of sin with the price paid in full by the precious blood of Christ. Any who add to this simple truth do not understand the 'precious' Blood.

Most diseases are directly traceable to the blood, confirming that *'the life'* indeed *'is in the blood'* (Leviticus 17:11). Through the sin of our first parents we were all born under the dominion of death.

But Jesus was, in this sense, different from us. His body was conceived apart from the seed of man, supernaturally conceived by the Holy Ghost. When He was born into this world He was called *'that holy thing'* (Luke 1:35). Mary's egg was not fertilized by the Holy Spirit, no, a thousand times *no*!

His body was entirely prepared by God in the virgin's womb. Hebrews 10:5 bears this out also: *'a body You have prepared for Me.'*

H.A. Maxwell White points out in *The Power of the Blood*, 'Mary was the chosen carrier of the body...' But the body itself and the blood that flowed in it were entirely made by the creative power of God. The Incarnation was a miracle!

Someone would object saying that His temptations would not be real to Him as ours are real to us, forgetting the fact that the first man, Adam, was created totally sinless and pure, too.

The blood that flowed in Jesus' body was pure blood, holy blood, innocent blood, living blood, and precious (rare) blood! It was and is *incorruptible blood* – not subject to moral or spiritual degeneration (see pages 200–205).

The Greek Meaning

The Greek word for 'precious'[5] is *timios* (#5093). In Thayer's Greek–English Lexicon it is defined thus:

    a. **held as of great price; i.e., precious**
    b. **held in honor, esteemed, especially dear**

Vine's gives us the same information: **costly, honorable, valuable, highly esteemed**.

Peter says, 'You were bought out of the slave market of sin with the costly, honorable, highly esteemed, and especially dear blood of Christ.' The blood of Jesus was the medium of exchange for our sin-debt.

We must adopt Peter's attitude toward the blood of Christ if we want God to teach us as He taught Peter. Deep inside your heart, worship the Lord as you say to Him:

    'Lord Jesus, Your blood is precious. I highly esteem and count as especially dear Your costly blood. I honor and hold as a great price the blood You poured out of Your body for my redemption and realize Solomon's expensive offering was but one cent in comparison with the value attached to Your blood sacrifice.'

Additional Notes

1. Because Araunah (Ornan in 1 Chronicles 21:14–30) was a Jebusite and not an Israelite, he may have freely offered the threshingfloor and oxen out of fear for his personal safety since he lived in Israel only by David's mercy (cf. Exodus 23:23). (The Jebusites were the earliest known inhabitants of Jerusalem.)

2. If Yahweh's anger was provoked toward Israel in the way they treated His servant Moses, insomuch that He threatened to wipe them out and make of Moses a great nation (see Exodus 32:7–14), then how much more was the heart of God moved when Jesus came unto His own and they received Him not! As the people mocked Christ they were mocking God: *'He who hates Me hates My Father also'* (John 15:23).

3. That Beelzebub (lord of the flies) hates the blood of Jesus is proof it is not common blood. Naturally, flies are drawn to the decaying blood of a recently bled corpse. Both Beelzebub and his 'flies' (demons) are repulsed by the incorruptible, precious blood of our Savior.

4. The tense of the Greek verbs in the passages in Revelation where we are told of a 'Lamb that had been slain' actually speak of a 'Lamb that has *just been slain*.' John's vision was more than 60 years after the crucifixion; yet, the sacrifice of Christ is most recent to the redeemed in heaven. The 'Eternal Spirit' (Hebrews 9:14) will see to this 'freshness' throughout the ages to come. The Sacrifice of the cross will never decrease in value in the redeemed's estimation or fade in beauty in their eyes.

5. Peter used this word three other times: of Jesus Himself (1 Peter 2:7); of our special faith (2 Peter 1:1); and of God's promises (2 Peter 1:4).

Questions on Chapter 1

1. What does the concept of 'sacrifice' mean in most minds?

   _____

   _____

2. Why did David refuse Araunah's generous offer and insist on buying it for a price?

   _____

   _____

3. What lesson can we learn from Solomon's great expense in providing 120,000 sheep and 22,000 oxen at the Temple dedication?

   _____

   _____

4. Give at least three meanings of the word 'precious' as used in 1 Peter 1:19.

   _____

   _____

5. Who created the blood in Jesus' body?

   _____

   _____

6. What did Paul and Peter say that Jesus used to purchase us from the slave market of sin?

   _____

   _____

7. Ask God to give you insight and spiritual
    illumination into the blood of Christ as being
    'precious' before you go any further in this study.
    What does 'precious' mean to you?

    _____

    _____

    _____

    _____

    _____

    _____

    _____

    _____

    (Compare your answer after you have completed
    the book.)

Chapter 2

Coats of Skins

'Also for Adam and his wife the LORD God made tunics of skin, and clothed them.'   (Genesis 3:21)

Have you ever wondered how clothes originated? Believe me, there is much more here than meets the eye!

Light Garments

'God (who) *is light'* also *'covers (Himself) with light as with a garment'* (1 John 1:5; Psalm 104:2). The Scripture seems to hint, perhaps, that Adam and Eve were initially clothed with divine presence like unto, say, the Shekinah glory. [1]

While they were naked in that they wore no material cloth, they must have been covered with a spiritual presence which hid their nakedness from their eyes. *'And they were both naked, the man and his wife, and were not ashamed'* (Genesis 2:25).

Our first parents were used to a covering of divine presence which disappeared the moment they sinned. (Our holy God cannot fellowship with sin.)

At the precise moment they partook of the forbidden fruit, sin entered the world. The author believes that the presence of God at once vanished. *'And the eyes of them both were opened* (uncovered), *and they knew* (or could see) *that they were naked . . . '* (Genesis 3:7).

Adam and Eve were used to a covering; consequently they hid themselves from God when they knew they were uncovered. First, they hid behind fig leaf aprons. Later they hid behind the trees. According to custom the Lord came into the garden, *'in the cool of the day'* that He might communicate with His favored creation. *'They looked unto Him and were lightened* (radiant)*'* was no doubt true of their daily experience (see Psalm 34:5).

Their fig leaf aprons could in no way compare with His glory coverings. Today it is the same – man's efforts to justify himself before God are nothing more than 'filthy rags' in His sight. [2]

Hide and Seek

When the tangible awareness of God's presence suddenly descends upon a meeting, two strikingly different reactions are immediately noticeable. Those who are in right relationship with God welcome His conscious Presence. Others are suddenly uncomfortable. They may squirm in their seats or get up and leave. Just like their first parents, it seems they want to hide themselves *'from the presence of the LORD God'* (Genesis 3:8).

Unconfessed sin always produces a barrier. Darkness always hides from light. *'For whatever makes manifest is light'* (Ephesians 5:13).

When the man and the woman hid themselves from God He did not destroy that which He had made in His own image and likeness. Rather, He sought His estranged creatures, calling out in the garden, *'Where are you?'* When man hides, God seeks.

Adam realized there was no use in hiding any longer. He reluctantly answered the divine summons, *'I heard Your voice in the garden and I was afraid because I was naked; and I hid myself'* (Genesis 3:10).

Adam was afraid because he was naked ... he was naked because he had sinned ... he clearly remembered what God had warned him:

> *'Of every tree of the garden you may freely eat; but of the tree of the knowledge of good and evil you shall not eat, for in the day that you eat of it you shall surely die.'* (Genesis 2:16, 17)

Standing before a holy God he was openly exposed with no covering. Before the God who made him, he trembled in fear awaiting his due punishment.

Substitution Death – The Great Exchange

God had clearly warned Adam *'... in the day that you eat of it you shall surely die.'* Until Adam sinned he had never seen death, because death only came into the world after Adam sinned (see Romans 5:12).

Death refers to **cessation**. When he ate of the fruit of the forbidden tree a 'death' occurred within him. A spiritual separation and loss of security registered inside. Was this inner cessation all God had meant when He warned *'you shall surely die'* or was something physical implied too?

As the man and the woman stood before God expecting His warning to be fulfilled, they must have been surprised by what God said. (You can read it in Genesis 3:16–19.) The punishment of hard labor was certain: he to produce bread and she to produce children. The expected death, however, did not occur that day at all![3]

The Lord told them instead that man would later return to the ground, that is, he would eventually die[4] (see Genesis 3:19).

Instead of immediate physical death, Adam soon found himself covered again ... but not with God's glory. This time he was covered with a coat of skin – and so was Eve.

This new covering was different from the former one. It was not made with, perhaps, the snap of a divine finger, but instead through a horrible and ugly occurrence. An animal (or animals) bled and died right before their eyes. How are we sure this occurred?

We are certain the 'skins' they were clothed with were **animal** skins because the Hebrew word infers that meaning. *Wilson's Old Testament Word Studies*, page 398, says the Hebrew word means **'the hide or skin of an animal: Gen. iii.21, &c.'**

It would be ludicrous to suggest that God supernaturally invented animal skins (without the animals) as He had formed the animals out of the ground in the early phases of the creation (see Genesis 2:19–20).

After killing the animal(s) God removed its skin from the dead body and presented it still warm and wet to our first parents. By this example the Lord impressed upon Adam and Eve the utter ugliness of sin and the wages it pays: **death**. With Adam and Eve thus clothed they were reckoned dead in the animal skins that covered them. In like manner, the Messiah's death provided payment for the penalty of sin and escape from its power. His cross, unlike modern jewelry crosses, was not a pretty sight. Jesus' death was **vicarious** (totally for another than Himself). His sinless life and substitutionary death was the Great Exchange for our sinful lives and eternal deaths. As Peter put it,

> 'For Christ also suffered once for sins, **the just for the unjust**, that He might bring us to God, being put to death in the flesh...'   (1 Peter 3:18)

Isaiah accurately foretold this ugliness – how Jesus would be *'marred more than any man and His form more than the sons of men'* and how He would have *'no form nor comeliness'* and how the onlookers would 'hide their faces from Him' (Isaiah 52:14; 53:2–3). Through the ugliness of His death, each person who accepts Him is clothed with the beautiful 'robe of righteousness' which His death provided.

Let us now examine six profound truths in this short verse of Scripture:

> 'Also for Adam and his wife the LORD God made tunics of skin, and clothed them.'   (Genesis 3:21)

There is a rule of interpretation in Bible study commonly known as **the law of the first mention**. This principle teaches that whenever any topic first appears in Scripture there are certain basic truths laid down in that first appearance which hold throughout the balance of Scripture, and upon which is built the complete revelation of that topic. The **first mention** of a topic is **foundational** to its further study. Although the words 'blood', 'substitution', and 'death' do not actually appear in this verse, the thoughts are readily apparent to the honest heart.

There are no fewer than seven foundational principles laid down in the last verse of the saddest paragraph in the Bible. They are:

1. God requires shedding of blood for sin.
2. The sinner must be covered with blood.
3. The life is in the blood.
4. God provides the sacrifice.
5. God Himself covers the sinner.
6. The innocent dies for the guilty.
7. God brings judgment upon the sacrifice.

1. God requires shedding of blood for sin

The Lord made 'coats of skins' from animal(s). In so doing its blood was shed and poured out on the ground. Shedding of blood was necessary to provide remission of transgression; '... *without shedding of blood is no remission* (forgiveness)' (Hebrews 9:22). **To be specific (and we should be) it is the *blood* that makes the atonement (or covering) for the sinner, not the *death* of the victim (which is the means to that blood).**

This is spelled out for us clearly in Leviticus 17:11:

> '*For the life of the flesh is in the blood: and I have given it to you upon the altar to make atonement for your souls: **for it is the blood that maketh an atonement** for the soul.*'

In recent years it has become popular to state that the blood of Jesus does not provide a covering (atonement) for the souls, but, rather a cleansing from sin. It is said the word 'atonement' itself is only an Old Testament word and concept and has no place in New Testament theology. I heartily concur that the blood of our Savior does provide a **cleansing**, but must also insist that a **covering** is provided as well.

That the statements of Paul and John on this matter could be overlooked (or ignored) is astonishing!

*'Whom God hath set forth to be a **propitiation** through faith in His blood...'*   (Romans 3:25)

*'And He is the **propitiation** for our sins...'*
(1 John 2:2)

The nouns Paul and John use in the literal Greek mean exactly what is rendered: ***propitiation***. What is most interesting here is the fact that the verb form (*hilaskomai*) is connected with the Hebrew word *kaphar* (the English word is 'atonement' in the Old Testament) by many Greek authorities (Vine, Unger, White, Thayer, etc.). The noun forms (*hilasmos* used by John and *hilasterion* used by Paul) have reference to ***the mercy-seat*** in the Old Testament tabernacle (the lid of the Ark of the Covenant). It was upon this 'mercy-seat' that the High Priest 'made atonement' for the nation of Israel by ***sprinkling blood*** upon it (see Leviticus 16). The Greek meaning 'signifies an expiation, a means whereby sin is covered and remitted' (W.E. Vine).

As our ***propitiation*** Jesus made Himself **an atoning sacrifice** at the cross and later carried His blood into the heavenly sanctuary (see Hebrews 9:11, 12, 24). Paul said that God made Jesus *'a **propitiation** (a mercy-seat) through faith in His blood.'* The Old Testament concept of **atonement** (*kaphar*), which means, 'to cover over, atone, propitiate, pacify' (*An Expository Dictionary of Biblical Words*, page 16), is realized in the New Testament term **propitiation**, which is why some authorities translate it as 'an atoning sacrifice.'

Rather than **atonement** being an obsolete word, found only in the Old Testament and abandoned in the New, the basic Old Testament meaning is fulfilled again and again in the New Testament (in Hebrews

2:17 it is translated *'to make reconciliation for the sins of the people'*).

God still requires **shedding of blood** to provide a **covering** that removes (expiates) the guilt of the sinner by **cleansing** away his sin. This logically leads us to the next foundational principle espoused by the first 'coats of skins'.

2. *The sinner must be covered with blood*

Not only was the substitute animal(s) slain, but its blood was applied to Adam and to his wife when God clothed them with its skins. The pouring out of blood provides a covering for the sinner, but the sinner must accept the sacrifice made on his behalf. Each individual must receive God's provision for himself. Jesus' blood was shed for the entire race of mankind. He is *'the Lamb of God who takes away the sin of the world'* (John 1:29). His sacrifice, however, must be accepted by each person, individually, or the death of Christ for that one is in vain.

Jesus shed His blood *for* us in order to give it *to* us. The elect are *'sprinkled'* with it (1 Peter 1:2), *'washed'* in it (Revelation 1:5), and *'made white'* by it (Revelation 7:14). His resurrected body no longer needs His blood – we need it.

When Thomas was told to put his finger into the print of the nails and thrust his hand into Christ's side, there was no possibility that he could have bloodied his hand, for there was not one drop of blood in the Savior's changed body [5] (1 Corinthians 15:50).

A fact we will make throughout this book is that the believer is covered with the blood of Christ. Our natural blood maintains the life of our body ... our spirit's life is maintained by Christ's blood. *'The life is in the blood.'* Jesus' blood was shed almost two milleniums ago, but is still efficacious for everyone who accepts Him. It is living blood and speaks to God from the mercy-seat in heaven on our behalf (see Hebrews 12:24).

3. *The life is in the blood*

Natural life is maintained by the blood that flows in a person's veins. Hence, *'For the life of the flesh* (physical life) *is in the blood...'*[6] Much of the sickness of the human race can be traced to the blood. Natural life is in our blood, and as we will see later, spiritual life is in the blood of Jesus. His body was made sovereignly of God (the word 'made' in Galatians 4:4 in the KJV is literally 'born'); His blood was made entirely by God's creative power. It had no stain of sin and carried no genetic defect in its chromosomes. *'A body You have prepared for Me'* the Logos exclaimed to God (see Hebrews 10:5) and the blood that flowed in that body was special blood (see Acts 20:28).

Jesus Christ so lived that He was the only man who never sinned, and was not worthy of its wages in any respect (see Hebrews 4:15; Romans 6:23; Luke 23:22).

Yet when Messiah laid down His life for us – for no man took it from Him – He did so by pouring out His blood (see John 20:11, 18 and compare to Leviticus 17:11). When He arose from the dead there was no blood in that changed body. Where is His blood now? The Bible teaches it has been sprinkled in two places:

Jesus' blood has been sprinkled on the mercy-seat in heaven:

> *'But you have come to Mount Zion and to the city of the living God, the heavenly Jerusalem ... and to the blood of sprinkling that speaks better things than that of Abel.'*   (Hebrews 12:22, 24)

Jesus' blood is sprinkled upon every child of God:

> *'Elect, according to the foreknowledge of God the Father, in sanctification of the Spirit, for obedience and **sprinkling of the blood of Jesus Christ**: Grace to you and peace, be multiplied.'* (1 Peter 1:2)

When Jesus' body was resurrected it was changed into a glorious state. The same skin and bones that were nailed to the cross were raised from the dead. Following His resurrection to a roomful of fearful disciples, our Lord said, *'Behold My hands and My feet, that it is I Myself: handle Me, and see; for **a spirit does not have flesh and bones as you see I have**'* (Luke 24:39). Some scholars have disputed this, misnoting 1 Corinthians 15:50 where Paul said *'Flesh and blood cannot inherit the kingdom of God.'* It is true *flesh* and *blood* cannot inherit the kingdom, but obviously *flesh* and *bone* can!

No one will go to hell because his sin has not been taken care of, but because he failed to personally accept the atonement.

After blood has been shed it must be ***applied***. This covering of blood is stated forthright in Leviticus 17:11:

> *'For the life of the flesh is in the blood: and I have given it to you upon the altar to make an atonement for your souls: for it is the blood that makes atonement for the soul.'*

Atonement is the Hebrew word *kaphar*, which means 'to cover and make reconciliation'. The phrase, 'it is the blood that makes an atonement' would mean, then, that only blood makes a covering which God accepts.

Bloodless coverings are unacceptable to God. **It is the blood that makes a covering for the person.**

4. *God provides the sacrifice*

In the first example of blood sacrifice God Himself made the provision and did not require the transgressors to provide it. Why did God do this in the first example? The answer can be seen in the fact that thousands of years later He provided the perfect sacrifice referred to as *'the Lamb of God'* and through His lamb He provided the *'robe of righteousness'* (individually) and *'garments of salvation'* (collectively) as Isaiah predicted. The 'coats of skins' He provided for Adam and Eve were types of the propitiatory covering in Messiah.

We have another example of God directly providing the sacrifice in the Old Testament. We have several key comments, but it will be necessary to record the entire account here with our comment following.

> '[1] *Now it came to pass after these things that God tested Abraham, and said to him, "Abraham!" And he said, "Here I am."*
> [2] *And He said, "Take now your son, your only son Isaac, whom you love, and go to the land of Moriah, and offer him there as a burnt offering on one of the mountains of which I shall tell you."*
> [3] *So Abraham rose early in the morning and saddled his donkey, and took two of his young men with him, and Isaac his son; and he split the wood for the burnt offering, and arose and went to the place of which God had told him.*
> [4] *Then on the third day Abraham lifted his eyes and saw the place afar off.*

[5] *And Abraham said to his young men, "Stay here with the donkey; the lad and I will go yonder and worship, and we will come back to you."*

[6] *So Abraham took the wood of the burnt offering and laid it on Isaac his son; and he took the fire in his hand, and a knife, and the two of them went together.*

[7] *But Isaac spoke to Abraham his father and said, "My father!" And he said, "Here I am, my son." And he said, "Look, the fire and the wood, but where is the lamb for a burnt offering?"*

[8] *And Abraham said, "My son, God will provide for Himself the lamb for a burnt offering." And the two of them went together.*

[9] *Then they came to the place of which God had told him. And Abraham built an altar there and placed the wood in order; and he bound Isaac his son and laid him on the altar, upon the wood.*

[10] *And Abraham stretched out his hand and took the knife to slay his son.*

[11] *But the Angel of the LORD called to him from heaven and said, "Abraham, Abraham!" And he said, "Here I am."*

[12] *And He said, "Do not lay your hand on the lad, or do anything to him; for now I know that you fear God, since you have not withheld your son, your only son, from Me."*

[13] *Then Abraham lifted his eyes and looked, and there behind him was a ram caught in a thicket by its horns. So Abraham went and took the ram, and offered it up for a burnt offering instead of his son.*

[14] *And Abraham called the name of the place The-LORD-Will-Provide; as it is said to this day, "In the Mount of the LORD it shall be provided." '*

(Genesis 22:1–14)

Verses 4–5

During the three days of travel to the mountain of sacrifice Abraham came to a new place of faith in God. Even though there was no precedent for resurrection, Abraham believed that Isaac, after he killed him, would be raised from the dead. This must have been his only conclusion since God had previously told Abraham that Isaac was the child of promise through whom Abraham would become the father of a multitude.

Therefore, if,

(a) God said Abraham must offer Isaac, and,

(b) Isaac was yet to father children (because God could not have lied about this fact), then,

(c) God would raise Isaac after Abraham offered him!

This was the greatest trial and exercise of Abraham's faith. In fact, the writer to the Hebrews refers to the offering of Isaac, rather than the birth of Isaac, as Abraham's faith trial:

> *'By faith Abraham, when he was tested, offered up Isaac, and he who had received the promises offered up his only begotten son, of whom it was said, "In Isaac your seed shall be called," concluding that God was able to raise him up, even from the dead, from which he also received him in a figurative sense.'* (Hebrews 11:17–19)

Abraham came to this conclusion during the three-day journey to Moriah. He instructed his servants to wait on them while he and Isaac went to the place of worship promising they both would return after they had offered the sacrifice!

Verse 7
This verse shows that children knew much about blood sacrifice as Isaac listed the items used, such as the fire and the wood, but asks his father about the lamb needed to offer a burnt offering. Parents trained their children about blood sacrifice by example and instruction, and passed this information down the generations until the Law was given.

Verse 8
A statement which reveals the nature of Jesus' sacrifice is: 'God will provide Himself a lamb.' Abraham did not end up slaying Isaac, his only begotten son through Sarah, but God did lay upon His Son the iniquity of us all (see John 1:29).

Verse 10
The ultimate test of Abraham's obedience. The knife would have gone into Isaac's chest had not the angel of the Lord called unto Abraham from heaven.

Verse 13
A ram caught in a thicket was the first fulfillment of the promise, 'God will provide Himself a lamb.' Jesus, the Lamb of God (from the Father's bosom) ultimately, perfectly, and absolutely fulfilled the promise. Ram (mature lamb) was offered *in the stead* of Isaac. Substitution principle once again enacted.

Verse 14
Abraham's revelation of Yahweh's redemption is explained in one of the many redemptive names of God given in the Old Testament. *'Jehovah-Jireh'* which means **The Lord will see (to it)**; or, as it is commonly taken to mean, **God supplies**.

5. *God Himself covers the sinner with the blood*

Notice in our text (Genesis 3:21) the phrase *'and clothed them'*, which could also be read *'and* (He) *clothed them'*. God not only provided the sacrifice and made the coverings of skins, but also clothed Adam and Eve with them. They did not clothe themselves. When it comes to the robe of righteousness and the garment of salvation. we do not put it on ourselves, but our Father dresses us. He clothes us with righteousness.

> *'I will greatly rejoice in the* LORD, *my soul shall be joyful in my God; for* **He hath clothed me** *with the robe of righteousness . . . '*   (Isaiah 61:10)

Paul expressed it in this manner, *'It is God that justifieth'* (Romans 8:33). We cannot do it ourselves, as sinners we call upon the Lord, but it is God who regenerates us on the basis of the blood of Christ.

6. *The innocent dies for the guilty*

The animal(s) the Lord slew in the stead of Adam and Eve had never done wrong or committed evil. They were innocent and yet they died. If this seems unfair think how much more 'unfair' that 'Christ died for the ungodly' (Romans 5:6). He was more than innocent, He was perfectly righteous. **Righteousness is innocence proven**. He was 'in all points tempted' and 'yet without sin' (Hebrews 4:15). The prince of the world (Satan) had not one legal claim on Him (John 14:30). Throughout the Bible sacrificial record **the guilt** of the transgressor is passed from himself to his sacrifice, and **the innocence** of the sacrifice or **righteousness** (in the case of Jesus) is transferred by imputation [7] to the transgressor.

Jesus foretold His offering of Himself in our place in Matthew 20:28:

> *'Even as the Son of man came not to be ministered unto, but to minister, and **to give His life a ransom for many**.'*

He gave Himself literally, 'a ransom for, or instead of, the many.'

7. *God brings judgment upon the sacrifice.*

In the first example it is obvious that the Lord Himself slew the sacrifice. Throughout the rest of the Old Testament either the sinner or the priest did the slaying. The 'first mention principle' once again points us to the New Testament, where Jesus experiences judgment on our behalf. Eight hundred years before Christ, Isaiah sees the crucifixion in progress and prophetically states in **past** tense,

> '... *the* LORD *hath laid on on Him the iniquity of us all* ... *Yet **it pleased the** LORD **to bruise Him;** He hath put Him to grief: when **Thou shalt make His soul an offering** for sin...'* (Isaiah 53:6, 10)

Paul, through the revelation given him, stated:

> *'For He* (the Father) *hath made Him* (the Son) *to be* (not in original) *sin* (or, 'a sin offering') *for us, who knew no sin; that we might be made the righteousness of God in Him.'* (2 Corinthians 5:21)

Jesus bore our sins in His **body on the tree** (1 Peter 2:24) abolishing the enmity in His **flesh** (Ephesians

35

2:15). At death His suffering was complete – and we now experience *'peace with God through our Lord Jesus Christ'* (Romans 5:1). Jesus made peace between God and man through the blood of His cross (see Colossians 1:20).

Adam and Eve's first encounter with substitutionary death and blood sacrifice was the foundation upon which they evidently offered animal sacrifices after they were excluded from the garden. Somehow, they knew this was necessary to approach the God whose holiness they had taken for granted. This information was passed from generation to generation long before the Law was given. Ancient man had a special reverence for blood sacrifice because God Himself had taught it to him when he first sinned. Abel came to God this way. Seth must have, too (see Genesis 4:26). Noah built an altar when he left the ark and received blessing for the 'new' earth (see Genesis 8:18–22). Job, which was probably the first book of the Bible actually written, offered animal sacrifices and so did his 'friends' (chapters 1, 42).

With so much biblical material about blood sacrifice it must be a paradox to any honest heart why so few ministers today, in any particular group or movement, espouse the merits of the precious blood of Christ.

Additional Notes

1. At the empty tomb 'two men ... in *shining garments*' appeared to the women who came to mourn. In Revelation 19:8 'the fine linen, clean and white' in which the saints are eternally arrayed is of a spiritual, rather than material quality. The linen is called 'the righteousness of saints'. The Gadarene demoniac 'wore no clothes' before Jesus delivered him, but afterwards was found 'clothed and in his right mind' (Luke 8:27, 35).

2. Man's good works, though noble and humanitarian, cannot achieve a right relationship with God, no matter how hard and long the works are performed. That the lost will be judged 'according to their works' (Revelation 20:12) proves this fact. No one's works are good enough to merit salvation. Jesus reproved those who 'trusted in themselves that they were righteous' (Luke 18:9).

3. This is not to say that Adam did not fully die 'in the day' that he sinned, as God had promised would happen, because a 'day is with the Lord as a thousand years' (2 Peter 3:8) and we read where 'all the days that Adam lived were nine hundred and thirty years: and he died' (Genesis 5:5).

4 These coats of skins covered their own physical skin. God made Adam's skin when He took him out of the ground and made Eve's when He took her from Adam's flesh (see Genesis 2:7, 21–24).

5. Notice also in John 20:25, 27 that the risen Christ does not have nail-*scarred* hands, as though they healed, but nail-*pierced* hands. (Jesus instructed Thomas to thrust his hand **into** His side.) Five of His wounds were left in His body when the Holy Spirit raised it from death (Romans 1:4) as eternal reminders that our exalted King was once a suffering Lamb. Forever Jesus Christ will bear the redemption marks in His glorious body – which our changed bodies that will be made like unto His will **not** bear.

6. The words 'life', 'soul', and 'souls' in Leviticus 17:11 are one word in the masoretic text: **nephesh**. It comes from *naphash* which means 'a breathing creature'. Long before science discovered the fact that the blood picks up the oxygen in the lungs and thus carries that life-giving element throughout the body, the Bible taught *'For the life of all flesh is the blood thereof'* (Leviticus 17:14). This *nephesh*, or life principle, was to be held sacred. When man killed animals for food he was to 'pour out the blood thereof and cover it with dust' (Leviticus 17:13) and it was never to be eaten with the flesh of the animal. The first prohibition against eating any manner of blood was given in the Noahic covenant (see Genesis 9:4) and was affirmed for the Church in Acts 15:20. The *nephesh* of man was especially sacred because man was made in the image of God. Whenever his blood was unjustly shed, it could only be silenced by the blood of the murderer. God Himself established capital punishment in Genesis 9:4–6 in His laws for man's government of himself. Without this law the way of all flesh would soon have corrupted himself again, as he had before the Flood: 'The earth

also was corrupt before God, and the earth was filled with violence' (Genesis 6:11). From Genesis (4:10) to Revelation (6:9–11) the blood of the murdered cries out to God for vengeance (compare to Hebrews 12:24).

7. To impute means 'to credit to one's account, to legally transfer from one to another'.

Questions on Chapter 2

1. Had you seen Adam and Eve in the garden before they sinned with what would they have been clothed?

   _____

2. When did they see that they were naked?

   _____

3. Why did they sew fig leaves together and make 'aprons'?

   _____

   _____

   _____

4. Why did God make coats of skins for them?

   _____

   _____

   _____

5. Since Adam and Eve already had physical bodies formed from the earth what types of 'skins' were these?

   _____

   _____

6. How did God get these skins for them? Did He just snap His finger, or was substitutionary death involved?

   _____

   _____

7. List at least four principles, based on the law of the first mention, from Genesis 3:21.

    _____

    _____

    _____

8. What did Isaac reveal concerning his knowledge of blood sacrifice in his question to his father about the need for a lamb, in addition to the wood and the fire?

    _____

    _____

9. Should parents teach their children godly principles today?

    _____

    _____

Chapter 3

Why God Accepted Abel's Offering

How *Not* to Win Friends

How could a God of love demand a blood sacrifice? The same serpent who influenced Cain puts the same ideas in people's heads today.

Many people scorn the blood sacrifice of Christ. Famous seminaries teach their ministerial students that the blood message is socially unattractive. Some 'ministers' label this message as 'the butcher shop gospel'.

'It insults my intelligence,' said one minister, 'that God could provide no better way to restore mankind than by nailing His own Son to the cross.' Such total ignorance of basic Bible truth is not new. Paul received similar objections from the philosophizing Grecian culture. He lamented their blind condition, observing that, '. . . *the cross is to those who are perishing foolishness.*'

Yes, the message of the cross is to those who perish utter foolishness. God, in His wisdom, has chosen *'the foolish things of the world to shame the wise,'* Paul says, and *'the foolishness of God is wiser than men'* (see 1 Corinthians 1:18–27 NASB).

The liberal theologians have always refused the blood truth. But what we find today are traditionally conservative theologians leaning toward the same mistake. Furthermore, we find charismatic and pentecostal leaders who downplay the necessity of the *blood* of Christ, emphasizing instead the necessity of His *death* (no matter how that death occurred). [1]

Several years ago an evangelical seminary purged some of its top professors. These particular theologians were purporting the idea that a literal devil did not exist, that Christ was not born of a virgin, and that His blood could not atone for sin.

Peter warns of *'false teachers'* who will craftily bring in *'damnable heresies'* (see 2 Peter 2:1). A damnable heresy is a teaching, which, if believed, will damn a person.

I was once cornered by a group of pentecostal preachers after I preached a simple message entitled 'Without Shedding of Blood'. I was hurt and grieved, not by their verbal attack upon me, but by their gross denseness concerning the importance of Christ **shedding His precious blood**.

I was invited to the pastor's home following the message and knew I was in trouble about something! The preachers, who had driven to the revival from the surrounding area, had whispered among themselves throughout my message. (I had noticed their actions while preaching and mistakenly thought they were whispering about my style of delivery or my credentials.)

As we sat down to sandwiches in the host pastor's home, the youngest of the ministers asked me, 'Did I hear you correctly tonight, Brother Alsobrook?'

'Correctly about what?'

'You said,' he continued, ' "if Jesus had not shed His blood we would be hopelessly lost." '

'That is what I said,' I replied unsure of his direction.

'Well, I'll have you know something for certain about the sacrifice of our Savior. Had He been strangled to death by frenzied Pharisees it would have sufficed for our salvation.'

Amazingly, **everyone else voiced their agreement with his statement!**

I looked in dismay at these ministers. Three of them were past middle age and had been in the ministry for years and years. It seemed totally unbelievable to me that men who professed such deeper life experiences (like the baptism with the Holy Spirit, for example) could believe that the shedding of Jesus' blood was **not** all-important for salvation.

Furthermore, the above was not an isolated incident. One of the damnable heresies in our time is that the blood does not atone. Usually one finds among 'full gospel' Christians a stricter adherence to the Word than is present in mainline churches. A decade ago, however, I was appalled at a popular trend among pentecostal preachers to de-emphasize the importance of blood sacrifice. During this period I was always traveling the country pointing out the obvious fallacy of such erroneous teaching. (This error spread like a plague for some years.) Countless times we pointed out that no sin offering could be made without blood under the Law (read Leviticus 4, 5, 6 and Hebrews 9:22). And that if Christ had been strangled by angry Pharisees we could not eat His flesh today (cf. Acts 15:19; 1 Corinthians 5:7–8; John 6:51–56).

In many of the mainline denominations songs which center around the blood of Christ have been deleted during continual hymnal revisions until one must look long to find perhaps one hymn extolling the virtues of the Blood. Liberal scholars have rendered the Greek

43

word *haima* as 'death' rather than 'blood' again and again throughout their spurious translations.

The forementioned examples clearly show how Satan is seeking to minimize the importance of Christ's blood. In Genesis 3 we have the first example of shedding of blood implied in verse 21 (as discussed in the previous chapter). **In the very next chapter** of Genesis (chapter 4) we see the first example of a man's refusal to come the way of blood sacrifice to God. The Apostle John later informs us that Cain's bloodless sacrifice was evil and that Cain himself was of the devil (see 1 John 3:12). Jude observed that false teachers in his day followed after *'the way of Cain'* in their teaching (Jude 11). The way of Cain is more prevalent in our day than it was in Jude's day. I believe I can make this statement based on actual observance, not hypothesis, throughout 14 years of frequent teaching about the Blood. I am no longer shocked by the misconception and ignorance of the Blood among America's clergymen, but I am continually grieved by their callousness, as the heart of God must surely be.

In Genesis 4, man's first attempt at his own religion is described for us. Humanism began when Cain attempted to approach God and find His favor the bloodless way. Cain's attempt ended in complete failure. How pitiably sad it is today that those who follow his **pattern** will end with his **punishment**. His isolation as a fugitive and a vagabond was symbolic of the eternally lost state of false worshipers.

Let's focus our attention upon the Scriptures for a verse by verse study of Genesis 4:1–13:

> *'Now Adam knew Eve his wife, and she conceived and bore Cain, and said, "I have gotten a man from the LORD."* [2] *Then she bore again, this time his*

brother Abel. Now Abel was a keeper of sheep, but Cain was a tiller of the ground. And in the process of time it came to pass that Cain brought an offering of the fruit of the ground to the LORD. Abel also brought of the firstlings of his flock and of their fat. And the LORD respected Abel and his offering, but He did not respect Cain and his offering. And Cain was very angry, and his countenance fell. So the LORD said to Cain, "Why are you angry? And why has your countenance fallen? If you do well, will you not be accepted? And if you do not do well, sin lies at the door. And its desire is for you, but you should rule over it." Now Cain talked with Abel his brother; and it came to pass, when they were in the field, that Cain rose against Abel his brother and killed him. Then the LORD said to Cain, "Where is Abel your brother?" And he said, "I do not know. Am I my brother's keeper?" And He said, "What have you done? The voice of your brother's blood cries out to Me from the ground. So now you are cursed from the earth, which has opened its mouth to receive your brother's blood from your hand. When you till the ground, it shall no longer yield its strength to you. A fugitive and a vagabond you shall be on the earth." And Cain said to the LORD, "My punishment is greater than I can bear!" '

(Genesis 4:1–13)

Conceived Once – Bore Twice

Notice the word 'conceived' appears once the above text while the word 'bore' appears twice. Throughout the Bible there are several examples of the recording of the conception with each birth. When a mother gives birth to two infants, after she has conceived one time, her children are twins. Notice the wording in Genesis 4:1–2. '... she bare Cain ... and again she bare his brother...' This would seem to suggest a possibility that these brothers were twins. If not, there could not have been a great age difference, as children's books sometimes show in the illustrations where Cain is full grown and bearded and his brother is smaller and smooth-faced. Each was involved in his own livelihood when the story occurs ... they must have been near each other's age.

The truth is these boys were men before they ever brought an offering to the Lord. *'And Abel was a keeper of sheep* (shepherd), *but Cain was a tiller of the ground* (farmer). *And **in process of time** it came to pass...'*

Abel and Cain were both occupied in a livelihood, grown up, and fully responsible. They were not irresponsible youths. A surface reading, coupled with tradition, often leads to a misconception about their age. The Bible skips twenty or more years between the first and second sentence in verse 2. Cain and Abel did not sacrifice until they were on their own. As children they were covered by their parents' offerings: *'... else were your children unclean; but now are they holy'* (1 Corinthians 7:14).

Even as early in the Scriptures as Genesis chapter 4, the Bible teaches the age of accountability (see also Jonah 4:11). As young adults, each had to bring his own sacrifice. Cain had to bring his for himself and Abel likewise (cf. Philippians 2:12). The phrase *'in the process of time'* further shows the time lapse involved. It can also be translated 'at the end of the days' perhaps referring to a particular season.

Hearing God's Word

Adam and Eve had learned from the coverings with which God had clothed them to shed the blood of an animal substitute whenever their conscience convicted them of sin. This was passed on to their offspring by example and instruction. Perhaps as they laid the lamb upon the rock they would say, 'Children, this is the way to remove the punishment of your evildoings.'

In later life Cain well knew he was rejecting God's method of approach when he offered fruit. These boys had grown into men watching their parents offer unto God animal sacrifices. They had heard their words of instruction concerning blood. Two scriptures bear out this point:

> *'By faith Abel offered unto God a more excellent sacrifice than Cain, by which he obtained witness that he was righteous.'* (Hebrews 11:4)

> *'So then faith cometh by hearing, and hearing by the word of God.'* (Romans 10:17)

If Abel offered his sacrifice to God by faith, and if faith comes by hearing the Word of God, how did Abel hear the Word of God?

Before we answer this question let's observe that Eve told the serpent what 'God hath said' in Genesis 3:2–3 (although she misquoted it), and yet when God said (in Genesis 2:16–17) the very words she referred to, she was not yet created! Notice, *'And the* LORD *God commanded **the man**, saying, Of every tree of the garden you may freely eat: But of the tree of the knowledge of good and evil, you shall not eat, for in the day that you eat of it you shall surely die.'* Only Adam was present

47

when God spoke these words. Eve was not created until later (Genesis 2:22). This would answer the question, 'How did Abel (as well as Cain) hear God's Word when they had no Bible, etc.?' From their father, Adam, of course. Just as Adam had previously taught God's commandment to Eve, they also trained their children in the way they should go – according to the instructions and example God had given them in the garden after they sinned. This is a biblical concept.

Offering the Curse

Modern scholars erroneously teach that both Abel and Cain were ignorant concerning sacrifices. They reason that Abel offered a lamb only because he was a shepherd and Cain offered fruit simply because he was a farmer. Such was not the case.

Cain knew he was rejecting God's only method of approach. Cain disbelieved the Word of God he had been taught by his parents. Cain's bloodless sacrifice was not due to ignorance; **it was a willful rejection of the divine revelation**.

No doubt his parents had told all their children (evidently Cain and Abel had unmentioned siblings) the full story of their sin in the garden and the resultant punishment God had placed on the woman and the man, and the curse He had placed on the serpent and on **the ground**. *'Cursed is the **ground** for thy sake ... thorns also and thistles shall it bring forth ... '* (Genesis 3:17–18). This fact clearly reveals the rebellious attitude Cain held toward God, for he offered what God had cursed, [3] in an attempt to receive blessing! It would have been better not to have offered anything than to bring the curse as an offering.

Cain openly flaunted God's method and mocked His

Word. The wonder is not that God sent no fire upon Cain's sacrifice, but that God sent no fire upon Cain! Even in this early period of time we see God's matchless mercy. **He even offered Cain a second chance:** *'If you do well,* (come God's way), *will you not be accepted?'* God beseeched Cain following his offering of grain (see Genesis 4:7). Cain still had opportunity to repent of his rebellion and offer to God the sacrifice of righteousness. God would have respected (accepted) an offering of blood from Cain just as He had from Abel, *'for there is no respect of persons with God'* (Romans 2:11).

The Fire Falls

It is difficult to completely write this in orderly fashion, since the exposition demands we get ahead of the order of events in an endeavor to bring forth each truth.

Go back to Genesis 4:3–5:

> *'And in the process of time* [4] *it came to pass that Cain brought an offering of the fruit of the ground to the Lord. Abel, also brought of the firstlings of his flock and of their fat. And the Lord respected Abel and his offering, but he did not respect Cain and his offering . . . '*

The questions posed by these verses are, In what way did God respect an offering? and, how was it that both sacrificers knew which sacrifice God accepted and which offering He refused?

We point out the obvious fact that there was an **open demonstration** that was clearly **supernatural**. This witness, or testimony of acceptance (see Hebrews 11:4), was openly manifest or **visible** to human sight.

There was no possibility of mistaking which offering God respected (accepted).

In repeated places the Old Testament states that God showed His acceptance of an offered sacrifice by sending fire from heaven and consuming it. Here are a few examples:

> *'And there came a fire out from before the 'LORD, and consumed upon the altar the burnt offering and the fat: which when all the people saw, they shouted, and fell on their faces.'* (Leviticus 9:24)

> *'Then the fire of the LORD fell, and consumed the burnt sacrifice . . . '* (1 Kings 18:38)

> *'Who when Solomon had made an end of praying, the fire came down from heaven, and consumed the burnt offering and the sacrifices; and the glory of the LORD filled the house.'* (2 Chronicles 7:1)

It is our conviction that *'. . . God testifying of his* (Abel's) *gifts . . . '* (Hebrews 11:4) refers to a **fire witness**[5] that involuntarily from human effort descended rapidly out of the sky upon the slain firstling of Abel's flock. This fire typifies one aspect of the Holy Spirit who falls in answer to the blood of Christ. Upon Cain's beautiful bouquet of luscious fruit there fell not even so much as a spark from above. A work of the flesh will never bring the blessing a sacrifice in the Spirit brings.

Another important observation from this particular passage points to the truth that *a person is either accepted or rejected on the basis of his sacrifice*. It was because God accepted Abel's sacrifice that He accepted Abel. Likewise, Cain was rejected because his sacrifice was rejected. Do not be misled into thinking Abel was automatically righteous prior to the sacrifice. Abel *'obtained witness that he was righteous,'* because he came offering God's way. Had he been sinless, he would have needed no sacrifice. Abel was just as much a sinner as Cain. The Word declares, *'All have sinned, and come short of the glory of God'* (Romans 3:23). One is accepted by God today only because the Sacrifice Himself is accepted.

Bloodless Religions Are Evil

Cain hated the blood because he was of the devil. *'Not as Cain, who was of the wicked one and murdered his brother. And why did he murder him? Because his works were evil, and his brother's righteous'* (1 John 3:12). The Apostle John tells us whose influence Cain was under when he offered his fruit. **Cain's bloodless sacrifice was due to satanic deception.**

When his offering was refused (God does not condone Satan's methods) and his brother's accepted, jealousy to the point of rage came over Cain. *'And Cain was very angry, and his countenance fell'* (Genesis 4:5). A spirit of anger entered into Cain's emotions, and a few days later a spirit of murder came in. Hatred always opens the door to murder if left unchecked. *'Whosoever hates his brother is a murderer'* (1 John 3:15), the apostle informs us only three verses after mentioning Cain's evil works.

Cain's hatred of Abel led to a premeditated plot to destroy his brother (cf. John 10:10). God saw it in Cain and tried to bring him to repentance.

'So the LORD said to Cain, "Why are you angry? And why has your countenance fallen? If you do well, will you not be accepted? And if you do not do

well, sin lies at the door. And its desire is for you, but you should rule over it."' (Genesis 4:6–7)

The Cain Spirit

It is hinted that Cain's attack upon Abel occurred sometime after the offering of the sacrifice.

> *'Now Cain talked with Abel his brother; and **it came to pass**, when they were in the field, that Cain rose against Abel his brother and killed him.'*
> (Genesis 4:8)

Isn't it interesting that the first anger and murder occurred on the basis of religion? In the Body of Christ today, **the Cain spirit** is moving forth in ever-widening circles. Brother rises up against brother, and through words kills the reputation of one Jesus loves. Malicious gossip, slander and backbiting are a few of the tools this spirit uses to accomplish its destructive task. Are you envious when another is moved to a higher position? Do you attack another's character without justifiable grounds?

Perhaps Satan moved into Cain's thought life weeks before this time when he realized that were he to offer a blood sacrifice he would have to obtain the lamb from his brother's flock. Or, maybe, as a boy watching the bleeding sacrifices die as his parents offered sacrifice to God, a seducing spirit would reason with his carnal mind saying, 'How unattractive!' When it came his time to go before God, something whispered to him, 'This beautiful bouquet would please God more.'

How true it is that blood sacrifice is ugly! It is not a beautiful picture at all. *'The wages of sin is death'* and was never meant to occur in God's beautiful creation.

If the devil ever tempts you to reject the blood of the cross on the basis that it is ugly, remind yourself: **so is sin**.

Through the ages, man's refusal of the blood is due to his refusal to acknowledge his sinfulness. Without blood sacrifice, however, there is no remission of sin (see Hebrews 9:22).

A Fugitive and a Vagabond

Banished from society and isolation from God was the punishment God placed on Cain. How true, yet sad, it is that all who reject God's provision in Jesus Christ are already banished from fellowship with Him now, and unless they repent will ultimately be isolated from God.

In Genesis 4:9 we see a prototype of the conscience. *Then the LORD said to Cain, Where is Abel your brother? And he said, I do not know. Am I my brother's keeper?'* Cain lied to God. *'And He said, what have you done? **the voice of your brothers blood**[6] cried out to Me from the ground'* (Genesis 4:10). Abel's blood cried unto the Lord from the ground. Jesus' blood cried unto the Father from the foot of the cross and still speaks to Him from the mercy-seat in heaven. The writer of Hebrews gives a parallel distinction between the cry of Jesus' blood and that of Abel's.

> *'And to Jesus the mediator of the new covenant, and to the blood of sprinkling, that **speaketh better things** than that of Abel.'* (Hebrews 12:24)

The *New International Version* says, *'speaks a better word.'* The better things or better word Christ's blood speaks is a word of **mercy**, whereas Abel's blood cried out for **vengeance**. **Judgment** fell on Cain for the blood of his brother, but **justification** comes to us today when we accept the blood of Jesus. Due to our transgressions Jesus was smitten. At this hour His blood is sprinkled upon the mercy-seat in heaven. Whenever we approach God and claim Jesus' work as our basis of access we have *'boldness to enter into the holiest'* (Hebrews 10:19).

The judgment which fell upon the first murderer was a rejection of his future toil upon the earth, and banishment as a wanderer upon the earth.

> *' "So now you are cursed from the earth, which has opened its mouth to receive your brother's blood from your hand. When you till the ground, it shall no longer yield its strength to you. A fugitive and a vagabond you shall be on the earth." And Cain said to the LORD, "My punishment is greater than I can bear!" '*
> (Genesis 4:11–13)

Yet, Cain's wandering as *'as a fugitive and a vagabond'* was only symbolic of the eternal wandering of a lost soul in outer darkness ... never able to find the door that leads home. Come God's way and be *'found of Him in peace, without spot, and blameless'* (2 Peter 3:14). Accept God's Lamb, who was offered as the perfect sin sacrifice for you, and make your robe *'white in the blood of the Lamb'* (Revelation 7:14).

He Being Dead Yet Speaketh

It was none other than our Lord Himself who designated Abel as a prophet (the first prophet, in fact) in Luke 11:50–51:

> *'That the blood of all the prophets ... From the blood of Abel unto the blood of Zacharias ... shall be required of this generation.'*

Yet, when we look at the Genesis record, we find no proof of a prophetic office in that young man's life; that is, no record of any utterance of divine origination is attributed anywhere to Abel.

But when we get to Hebrews, we find that Abel, who is dead, still speaks (Hebrews 11:4) and that Jesus' blood says something better than Abel's blood ever said (Hebrews 12:24). After contemplating all the above for quite some time, it came to me one day – Abel was a prophet in that he spoke on God's behalf concerning the merit of blood sacrifice and the persecution that comes from the world for the Blood! He prophesied, in the offering of his firstlings, that God would provide a Lamb for man, but that mankind, in large part, would refuse God's gracious provision and would despise those who welcome God's remedy for their sin.

Jesus told His disciples, *'If the world hates you, you know it hated Me before it hated you'* (John 15:18). John said, *'Marvel not, my brethren if the world hate you'* only one verse after he said, *'Cain, who was of that wicked one ... slew his brother'* (1 John 3:12–13). Cain, the father of false religion, hated Abel, the embodiment of pure religion. Abel, the offerer of blood sacrifice, sealed his testimony with his own blood, *'and by it he being dead yet speaketh'* (Hebrews 11:4).

Additional Notes

1. Let me quote from two scholars of the previous century whose insights on the importance of the **blood** in the making of atonement are noteworthy:

'For the **death** of the sacrifice was only a means toward an end; that end being the shedding and sprinkling of the **blood**, by which the atonement was really made.'   (Alfred Edersheim in *The Temple, Its Ministry and Services*, p. 88)

'All the detailed requirements of the Mosaic ritual ... go to show the pre-eminence of the **blood** of the sacrificial offerings; go to show, that it is the **life** (which the blood is), and not the **death** (which is merely necessary to the securing of the blood), of the victim, that is the means of atonement...'

(H. Clay Trumbull in *The Blood Covenant*, p. 245)

2 Perhaps Eve thought her firstborn son was 'the seed' that God promised would crush the serpent's head. Genesis 3:15 is the first messianic prophecy and Genesis 4:1 is the first misinterpretation of messianic prophecy (if such is the case).

3 The curse God spoke on the ground was most likely only twenty years or so earlier. The curse on the ground was **legally** removed after Noah disembarked and offered sacrifice (see Genesis 8:21). It will be **physically** and totally realized when Jesus Christ literally reigns on the earth (see Isaiah 55:13; Romans 8:19–22).

4. It can also be translated 'at the end of the days' perhaps referring to the growing season. (Genesis 8:22 may imply seasons did not begin until after the Flood.)

5. For more study on the subject of the fire of God, write for our book, *Have You Ever Heard of Heavenfire?'*

6. Because the life principle, or *nephesh*, is in the blood (Leviticus 17:11), that blood cries out to the Creator for vengeance whenever it is unjustly shed – even the blood of Christians (see Revelation 6:9, 10). Perhaps Stephen's blood did not cry out for vengeance, due to his special request and possession by the Spirit of Christ (Acts 7:60).

Questions on Chapter 3

1. In what ways does Satan de-emphasize the importance of the Blood today?

   _____

   _____

   _____

2. What is the first example in the Bible of man's attempt to approach God with a bloodless sacrifice?

   _____

   _____

3. Could it be possible that Cain and Abel were close in age?

   _____

   _____

   _____

   _____

4. How is it that Abel received faith to offer a more excellent sacrifice than Cain?

   _____

   _____

   _____

5. Did Cain realize he was approaching God in the wrong way? Did he operate out of ignorance or rebellion?

   _____

6. Give one or more examples of God's mercy toward Cain.

_____

_____

_____

7. How did the sacrificers know which sacrifice God accepted and which one He refused?

_____

_____

8. Did John imply that Cain was sincere but ignorant?

_____

9. Who were the influences in Cain actually coming from?

_____

10. Where does the Scripture teach that blood sacrifice is 'righteous'?

_____

_____

11. Over what issue was the basis of the first murder?

_____

_____

12. What is Cain's banishment figurative of today?

_____

_____

13. Did the literal blood of Abel exhibit any unusual quality when it was shed?

_____

_____

_____

14. In what way does the blood of Christ speak differently than Abel's blood?

_____

_____

Chapter 4

Lamb Requirements

It has been said that Jesus is equated with the concept of a **lamb** some thirty-three times in the Bible. Although some of the references are to the literal sheep sacrificed in the Old Testament (which foreshadow Christ), this is an amazing thought! It is commonly accepted that our Lord was precisely the age of 33 when He was offered for us on the cross.

We can look in the Law and see that Moses' use of the lamb for sacrifice did indeed picture the nature of Jesus and the qualifications required of Him as the Lamb of God.

The Lamb Must Be Perfect

The Passover Lamb, which marked the beginning of the exodus of Israel from Egypt, could not have a blemish on it anywhere. *'Your lamb shall be without blemish, a male of the first year...'* (Exodus 12:5). Later in Leviticus 22:20 a law of sacrifices reads, *'But whatever has a defect, you shall not offer, for it shall not be acceptable on your behalf.'*

In His instructions about the feast of the firstfruits the Lord says through Moses,

> *'And you shall offer on that day, when you wave the sheaf, a male lamb of the first year without blemish, as a burnt offering to the LORD.'* (Leviticus 23:12)

This offering typifies the resurrection of our Lord.

> *'But now Christ is risen from the dead, and has become the firstfruits of those who have fallen asleep. . . . But each one in his own order: Christ the firstfruits; afterward those who are Christ's at His coming.'* (1 Corinthians 15:20, 23)

Jesus fulfilled these requirements given in the Law. He was a male, a man *'of the first year'* – in the prime of life and perfect in spirit, soul and body. Peter tells us we are not redeemed with corruptible things, *'But with the precious blood of Christ, as of a lamb without blemish and without spot'* (1 Peter 1:19).

Physically, Jesus was without blemish. He was a perfect man. Because He never sinned, He was not worthy of death and not subject to its forerunner: sickness. His acquaintance with sickness and pain all took place within the last few hours of His natural life. During the thirty-three years He walked among men He was the perfect specimen of health. The body of the last Adam was just as sovereignly created by God in the womb of Mary as was the body of the first Adam formed by God from the clay. He had no sin until sin was legally laid upon Him at the cross, neither any sickness until He bore ours at the whipping post. Prior to the Fall, the first Adam had a natural body that was sinless and sickless until he disobeyed God. Sickness entered into the first Adam's flesh only after sin.

How can we be certain that sickness entered the

world because of sin? A picture of this truth is given to us in the saddest chapter in the Bible – Genesis 3. In verse 14 God said the serpent *and you shall eat dust'* immediately prior to telling the man *'for dust you are, and to dust you shall return'* (Genesis 3:19).

Our thinking is that God gave legal permission to Satan to afflict with sickness the physical body of disobedient man in Genesis 3 as a direct consequence of sin. This sickness allowance would permit the enemy to afflict man with the sting of death, inasmuch as sickness and death have been associated together throughout the annals of history.

The good news is that the head of the serpent was crushed by the Seed of the woman (Jesus Christ) as foretold in Genesis 3:15. It is impossible for a snake to eat with its head crushed!

Jesus was 'without spot' spiritually. He 'was in all points tempted like as we are, yet without sin' (Hebrews 4:15). He 'knew no sin' by transgression (2 Corinthians 5:21). He was 'holy, harmless, (and) undefiled' (Hebrews 7:26). Satan tried every trick on Jesus that he ever tries on anyone. Today we have no excuse if we do not overcome as Jesus overcame, for He has provided all the necessary equipment. Jesus was the perfect lamb.

The Lamb Was to Be a Sin Offering

Throughout the Word we see the lamb offered instead of the sinner. Abel's sheep atoned for Abel's sin. Isaac's lamb was offered *'in the stead'* of Isaac. The Law made provision for bringing *'a lamb for a sin offering'* (Leviticus 4:32). The Lamb of God is *'the propitiation for our sins'* (1 John 2:2).

The Lamb Had to Be Slain

The law of cleansing lepers specifically instructed, *'And the priest shall take one male lamb, and offer it as a trespass offering ... And he shall kill the lamb...'* (Leviticus 14:12–13). Isaiah prophesied concerning Christ saying, *'... He was cut off out of the land of the living...'* (Isaiah 53:8). John heard *'the voice of many angels ... saying with loud voice, Worthy is **the Lamb that was slain** to receive power, and riches, and wisdom and strength and honour, and glory, and blessing'* (Revelation 5:11–12).

A Lamb for the World

In the Old Testament we see **a lamb for a man** in many examples: Genesis 4:4, 22:13; Leviticus 14:11–14 and many others. The Passover pictures **a lamb for a house** (family).

> *'Speak to all the congregation of Israel, saying: on the tenth day of this month every man shall take for himself a lamb ... **for a household.**'* (Exodus 12:3)

The Day of Atonement demonstrated the offering of **a lamb for a nation**: see Leviticus 16:29–34, 23:26–32; Hebrews 9:7, 25. Each of these point to Jesus.

It is not until the New Testament, however, that we see **a lamb for the world.**

> *'The next day John saw Jesus coming toward him, and said, Behold! The Lamb of God, who takes away **the sin of the world.**'* (John 1:29)

Do you see the circle ever widening? It begins with a

lamb for a man, spreads to a lamb for a house, increases to a lamb for a nation (Israel), and ultimately finishes in **a lamb for the world**. Jesus is the ultimate Lamb. His sacrifice is greater than that of calves and sheep.

So perfectly perfect and completely complete is His offering of Himself that He could say of His work, *'It is finished'* (John 19:30). **There is no further need for any more blood sacrifices.** His sacrifice accomplished the will of the Father in removing sin from the very conscience of the worshiper (see Hebrews 9:13–14). It will never be repeated...

> *But this Man, after He had **offered one sacrifice for sins** forever, sat down at the right hand of God.'*
> (Hebrews 10:12)

Questions on Chapter 4

1. How many times is Jesus referred to
    prophetically in the Old Testament and
    specifically in the New Testament as a lamb?
    What is the significance of this number?

    _____

    _____

    _____

2. What relationship was there between the levitical
    requirements of lamb sacrifice and our Lord
    Jesus?

    _____

    _____

    _____

    _____

3. Was Jesus perfect in body (physical health and
    characteristics) during His natural life?

    _____

    _____

    _____

4. In the Old Testament the lamb was offered for
    sin and trespass offerings. What did John the
    Baptist say of Christ that would point to this?

    _____

    _____

    _____

5. Define the progression of lamb sacrifices in relationship to their atoning significance and their fulfillment in Christ.

    _____

    _____

    _____

    _____

    _____

Chapter 5

The Protection of the Blood

The tenth and final plague brought against the Egyptians which resulted in Israel's deliverance from the Pharaoh's rule was *'the death of the firstborn.'* Yahweh promised, *'And all the firstborn in the land of Egypt shall die, from the firstborn of Pharaoh who sits on his throne, even unto the firstborn of the maidservant who is behind the handmill, and all the firstborn of the beasts'* (Exodus 11:5).

Even up to the dreadful ninth plague of locusts Pharaoh had repeatedly hardened his heart and refused to release the children of Israel. Each plague was more severe than its predecessor. The final plague's death of the firstborn would be so horrible that as God told Moses, *'... there shall be **a great cry** throughout all the land of Egypt, such as there was not like it before, nor shall be like it again'* (Exodus 11:6). The sorrow of this plague upon Pharaoh would cause the stubborn monarch to not only, *'let you go, he will surely drive you out of here altogether'* (Exodus 11:1).

God provided a way of escape from the plague for all who would believe the commandment Moses gave and follow the instructions. This provision of protection for believing Hebrews was called 'The Passover' and became their yearly memorial feast of deliverance. Note the relevance from the passage in Exodus 12 for us today:

> *'Speak ye unto all the congregation of Israel, saying, In the tenth day of this month they shall take to them every man a lamb, according to the house of their fathers, a lamb for an house.'*
>
> (Exodus 12:3)

It was each father's duty to provide a lamb for his family's protection. (See Acts 16:31 for a New Testament similarity.)

> *'And if the household be too little for the lamb let him and **his neighbor next unto his house** take it according to the number of the souls; every man according to his eating shall make your count for the lamb.'* (Exodus 12:4)

Sharing the lamb with his neighbor pictures the believer sharing the Lamb of God with his friends.

After Christ told the Samaritan woman the secrets of her life, she went into the city and said, *'Come, see a man, which told me all things that I ever did: is not this the Christ?'* (John 4:29). Thus she shared the Lamb with her neighbors who later responded, *'Now we believe, not because of thy saying for we have heard Him ourselves, and know that this is indeed the Christ, the Savior of the world'* (John 4:42).

The early Christians *'(broke) bread from house to house ... Praising God ... And the Lord added to the church daily such as should be saved'* (Acts 2:46–47). It was as they shared Jesus with their neighbors that the Lord added to the Church on a day-by-day basis.

> *'Your lamb shall be without blemish, a male of the first year: ye shall take it out from the sheep, or from the goats.'*   (Exodus 12:5)

(Chapter 4, 'Lamb Requirements' shows how Jesus perfectly fits this type.)

> *'And ye shall keep it up until the fourteenth day of the same month: and the whole assembly of the congregation of Israel shall kill it in the evening.'*
>   (Exodus 12:6)

The last half of the time that Jesus was dying on the cross the synoptic Gospels all declare that a **supernaturally-created darkness** hung over the land.

> *'And it was about the sixth hour* (noon), *and there was a darkness **over all the earth** until the ninth hour* (3 pm). *And **the sun was darkened**...'*
>   (Luke 23:44–45; Matthew 27:45; Mark 15:33)

Because God's Word states *'the sun was darkened'* and because Luke specifically tells us that this darkness hovered *'over all the earth'* we must reject the notion that the darkness was caused by huge numbers of evil spirits hovering over Jerusalem while Jesus hung dying on the cross.

> *'And they shall take of the blood, and strike it on the two **side** posts and on the **upper** door post of the houses, wherein they shall eat it.'*   (Exodus 12:7)

Notice, God did not mention the threshold of the door at all. Do not regard the blood of Christ as an unholy thing fit only to trample underfoot. Consider the following verse:

> *'Anyone who has rejected Moses' law dies without mercy on the testimony of two or three witnesses. Of how much worse punishment do you suppose, will be be thought worthy who has trampled the Son of God underfoot, counted the blood of the covenant by which he was sanctified a common thing, and insulted the Spirit of grace?'* (Hebrews 10:28–29)

What does the above verse teach us?

First: Those who reject the blood of the new covenant will suffer a 'much sorer punishment' than those who despised Moses' law. The penalty for rejecting the law under the old covenant was *'death without mercy'* (see Numbers 15:30–31; Deuteronomy 17:2–6). The penalty for treading Jesus underfoot, counting the blood unholy, and despising the Holy Spirit is much sorer than physical death – it is an eternal death (see Revelation 21:8, 27).

Second: Just as the law despisers suffered death without mercy in the old covenant, there will be no mercy for those who die despising Jesus' sacrifice.

> *'For we know Him that hath said, Vengeance belongeth unto me, I will recompense, saith the Lord. And again, The Lord shall judge His people. It is a fearful thing to fall into the hands of the living God.'* (Hebrews 10:30–31; see also 9:27; 12:25)

Third: This judgment will come on those who in time past 'were sanctified'. Notice, this mocker will be thought worthy of eternal punishment because he now counts the blood *'wherewith* (in time past) *he was* *sanctified'* an unholy, disgraceful thing. This would indicate that sanctified people can apostatize to a place of final rejection by God. At one time they did accept Christ's blood as their atonement, otherwise they could not have been sanctified by it. Later, through satanic influence, they completely disregarded (as common and unclean) Jesus' blood. When a person absolutely rejects Jesus' sacrifice, there remains no other sacrifice for sin (see Hebrews 10:26), and he will have to suffer punishment of such rejection.

A willful apostate, however, is different from a common backslider. The apostate rejects the truth that Christ's blood can save. As long as the backslider retains his faith in the atonement of Christ, he can be renewed through sincere repentance (see James 5:20).

> *'And they shall eat the flesh in that night, roast with fire, and unleavened bread; and with bitter herbs they shall eat it.'* (Exodus 12:8)

> *'Eat not of it raw, nor sodden at all with water, but roast with fire; his head with his legs, and with the purtenance thereof.'* (Exodus 12:9)

Eating the flesh of the passover lamb symbolizes eating the flesh (partaking of) Christ. Note John 6:52–58:

> *'The Jews therefore quarreled among themselves, saying, "How can this Man give us His flesh to eat?" Then Jesus said to them, "Most assuredly, I say to you, unless you eat the flesh of the Son of Man and drink His blood, you have no life in you. Whoever eats My flesh and drinks My blood has*

eternal life, and I will raise him up at the last day. For My flesh is food indeed, and My blood is drink indeed. He who eats My flesh and drinks My blood abides in Me, and I in him. As the living Father sent Me, and I live because of the Father, so he who feeds on Me will live because of Me. This is the bread which came down from heaven – not as your fathers ate the manna, and are dead. He who eats this bread will live forever."' '

Jesus was not a cannibal. There was no way the Jews who heard Him could take this statement to mean that. They knew from the Law that eating was figuratively used of partaking. In Proverbs 9:17 and Hosea 10:13 eating is spoken figuratively as partaking of evil. In the New Testament eating is used as one way of symbolically partaking of spiritual food. Of Israel Paul says, *'And did all eat the same spiritual meat'* (1 Corinthians 10:3). James speaks figuratively that cankered gold and silver shall *'eat your flesh'* (James 5:3). Christ spoke prophetically, *'For the zeal of Thine house hath eaten Me up . . . '* (Psalm 69:9). In John's vision he ate a book – *'And I took the little book out of the angel's hand, and ate it up . . . '* (Revelation 10:10).

Neither did Jesus mean that they must literally drink His blood. The Jews once again should have understood He meant they were to spiritually partake of His blood. They had no excuse to be offended at His words. This figure of speech was common at the time. None of Jesus' followers took this statement literally for none of them (the women and John) at the foot of the cross drank His blood. This would have been an abomination in the sight of God for He has laid down a rule He has never revoked.

> *'Moreover ye shall eat **no manner of blood** ... what-soever soul it be that eateth any manner of blood, even that soul shall be cut off from his people.'*
> (Leviticus 7:26–27)

A clue to properly understanding what Jesus meant is seen in John 6:51:

> *'I am the living bread ... if any man eat of this bread, he shall live forever: and the bread that I give is my flesh, which **I will give for the life of the world.**'*

Believing what He did upon the tree, then, would be partaking or eating of His flesh. In the act of giving His flesh for the life of the world He has provided His flesh and His blood for the believer in which to freely partake. Christ instituted the 'Lord's Supper' (see 1 Corinthians 11:20) that the church might partake of the elements of bread and fruit of the vine and spiritually eat His flesh and drink His blood. Notice how Paul likens the communion to Israel's eating of the sacrifices:

> *'The cup of blessing which we bless, is it not the communion of the blood of Christ? The bread which we break, is it not the communion of the body of Christ? For we, being many, are one bread and one body, for we all* (the church) **partake of that one bread** (Christ). *Observe Israel after the flesh: are not these who **eat of the sacrifices** partakers of the altar?'* (1 Corinthians 10:16–18)

The communion (fellowship, sharing) of the Blood and Body are represented in the fruit of the vine and bread. In John 6:51 Christ said, '... *the bread* ... *is My flesh* ... ' Therefore eating His flesh is eating the bread which we bless in the Lord's Supper. Drinking His blood is drinking the juice in the cup which we bless. When a believer understands the Lord's Supper and partakes of the elements in faith, there is a spiritual fellowship with the Lord and with fellow members of Christ's body. The blood of Christ and the flesh that bore stripes for our healing enter into the believer by the Spirit and are manifest in his mortal body. There is healing in the communion.

Matthew's account of the Lord's Supper, instituted at the last supper Christ ate with His disciples, is the most endearing to me of the four accounts in the New Testament (see Matthew 26:26–30; Mark 14:22–25; Luke 22:14–20; 1 Corinthians 11:23–29).

> *'And as they were eating, **Jesus took bread** and blessed it, and brake it, and gave it to the disciples, and said, Take, eat; **this is My body**. And He took the cup, and gave thanks, and gave it to them, saying, **Drink ye all of it**; For **this is My blood** of the new testament, which is shed for many for the remission of sins.'* (Matthew 26:26–30)

'As they were eating' points out the fact that the communion naturally flowed into being. It was not a starchy meeting, but a friendly and informal communing in the love of God. *'Jesus **took** bread, and **blessed** it, and **brake** it, and **gave** it* ... ' He took, He blessed, He brake, and He gave. These four steps follow in progressive order in the lives of each of His disciples. He takes us into His arms when He saves us. He blesses us with the Holy Spirit. He breaks us at the cross. He gives us to others in ministry. We enjoy so much His taking and

74

blessing of our lives, but we must experience the breaking of our self-life before He can give us to His Body as a ministry gift.

Concerning the broken bread He said, *'Take...'* We must receive what He gives. The broken bread represents the scourged and marred body offered for our healing (see Isaiah 53:5; 1 Peter 2:24). *'... eat; this is My body.'* The bread eaten in faith ministers His flesh to us. He gave thanks for the cup saying, *'Drink you all of it* (everyone of you drink it)*; For this is My blood...'*

Do you follow His pattern of giving thanks for the cup by giving thanks to Him for His blood? **Do you thank God for the blood of Christ?** Notice in this text the two verbs indicating what each believer must do: eat and drink. The child of God must eat Christ's flesh and drink His blood.

Now, back to our discussion of the Passover. The children of Israel were instructed to eat the flesh of that first passover lamb. The exodus (departure) from Egypt would begin that very night and they needed the strength that lamb afforded. However, there appears to be more than a natural strengthening in their bodies in the meat of the passover lamb. Exodus 13:21-22 teaches us that the whole nation of Israelites walked at least one full day and one full night, without rest or food provision, which was a feat of considerable endurance for the elderly and the very young.

The author believes that the first passover meal ministered supernatural strength and healing to their entire race, while the blood from each passover lamb protected the oldest son from certain death. Behind closed doors, sprinkled with blood probably three million Israelites partook of the flesh of the roasted sheep. Under the covering of blood they hurriedly ate as much meat as they possibly could, knowing that any of it which remained had to be destroyed at daybreak. Among these millions throughout Goshen (the segregated area of Egypt where the Hebrews lived in poverty) were thousands of sick and diseased persons, yet a few hours later *'there was not one feeble* (weak, sick) *person among their tribes'* (Psalm 105:37). [1]

The greatest mass miracle service that ever occurred took place behind closed doors as the children of Israel ate the lamb's flesh. The strength they received from that one meal was so great that they traveled *'by day and night'* for at least one or two days without exhaustion (see Exodus 13:21). When we partake by faith of Jesus' flesh the same thing occurs today, *'For even Christ our passover* (lamb) *is sacrificed for us'* (1 Corinthians 5:7).

They were to eat the lamb *'roast*(ed) *with fire...'* Fire pictures God's acceptance of Christ as in the Old Testament where fire showed God's acceptance of the sacrifice. They were told not to eat it raw (later all uncooked meats were forbidden); God was showing them the break the Israelites must make with all the ways of Egypt. Fire speaks of judgment which Jesus legally took for us. The Passover lamb was not to be *'sodden* (boiled) *at all with water'* since water is a type of life and the Perfect Lamb *'tasted death for every man'* (Hebrews 2:9).

Unleavened Bread

They were to eat the flesh with unleavened bread. We are to partake of the Lamb with purity, sincerity, and truth. It is most important to see in the Word what leaven represents. Leaven typifies iniquity, false doctrine, hypocrisy, uncleanness, and legalism.

First: Leaven bread was never to be offered in a blood sacrifice.

> *'Thou shalt not offer the blood of My sacrifice with leavened bread...'* (Exodus 23:18)

Second: No burnt offering was to be made with leaven.

> *'No meat offering, which ye shall bring unto the LORD, shall be made with leaven: for ye shall burn no leaven, nor any honey, in any offering of the LORD made by fire.'* (Leviticus 2:11)

Third: Jesus pictured the corruption of the kingdom in this age to the fermentation of leaven.

> *'Another parable spake He unto them; The kingdom of heaven is like unto leaven, which a woman took, and hid in three measures of meal, till the whole was leavened.'* (Matthew 13:33; see also Luke 13:21)

He was showing by this parable that the church age would be filled with false doctrine and impurity that would pollute the truth and ministry of the kingdom. As false doctrine began to enter the Church toward the end of the first century AD, it grew and multiplied until at this hour we can easily observe *'the whole* (is) leavened'. Paul warned the church at Galatia that the legalistic persuasion of false doctrine they were accepting was not from God. He reminded the early Christians, *'A little leaven leaveneth the whole lump'* (Galatians 5:9).

On this same line Jesus warned His disciples, *'Take heed and beware of the leaven of the Pharisees and of the*

Sadducees' (Matthew 16:6). The disciples, whose hearts were hardened, misunderstood Christ. They reasoned among themselves, '...*It is because we have taken no bread'* (Matthew 16:7). Jesus told them, '*I spake it not to you concerning bread...* ' (Matthew 16:11). *'Then understood they how that He bade them not beware of the leaven of bread, but of the doctrine of the Pharisees and of the Sadducees'* (Matthew 16:12). Leaven speaks figuratively of false doctrine of which we are to *'beware'* (see also Mark 8:14–21).

Fourth: Our Lord's fourth truth illustrated by leaven concerns hypocrisy.

> *'In the meantime, when there were gathered together an innumerable multitude of people, insomuch that they trode one upon another, He began to say unto His disciples first of all, Beware ye of the leaven of the Pharisees, **which is hypocrisy**. For there is nothing covered, that shall not be revealed; neither hid, that shall not be known.'* (Luke 12:1–2)

Religious play-acting is also symbolized by leaven. Nominal churches today are filled with such leaven in their so-called 'worship services' during which they follow a printed program rather than the moving of the Holy Spirit. Pentecostal/charismatic churches major on the leaven of soulish entertainment.

Fifth: Leaven typifies lust (Hosea 7:4). The church of Corinth was infected with uncleanness that even the heathen had no name for. A man living with his father's wife! Rather than mourning over this sad condition and seeking to rectify it, the Corinthians were puffed up (see 1 Corinthians 5:1–5). As Paul ministers the necessary church discipline, he rebukes them saying,

> *'Your glorying is not good. Know ye not that a little leaven leaveneth the whole lump? Purge out therefore the old leaven, that ye may be a new lump, as ye are unleavened. For even Christ our passover is sacrificed for us: Therefore let us keep the feast, not with old leaven, neither with the leaven of malice and wickedness; but with the unleavened bread of sincerity and truth.'* (1 Corinthians 5:6–8)

The *'leaven of malice and wickedness'*, sad to say, is prevalent within the ranks of the Church in this final hour.

If we do not obey the command *'to purge out ... the old leaven'* we will not be *'a new lump'* the Master will honor. Leaven represents evil and sin. Observe that Israel could not eat the lamb without unleavened bread. Neither can the believer partake of Christ while holding to false doctrine, hypocrisy, and sin. We must purge ourselves from these that we might feast at His table. *'Let every one that nameth the name of Christ depart from iniquity'* (2 Timothy 2:19).

> *'You shall let none of it remain until morning, and what remains of it until morning you shall burn with fire.'* (Exodus 12:10)

This teaches us that there is a limited time that the Christian may experience growth in God and when it is over, **it is over!**

> *'For we must all appear before the judgment seat of Christ: that every one may receive the things done in the body, according to that he hath done, whether good or bad.'* (2 Corinthians 5:10)

> *'And thus you shall eat it: with a belt on your waist, your sandals on your feet, and your staff in your hand. So you shall eat it in haste. It is the LORD's Passover.'* (Exodus 12:11)

The first part of this verse corresponds with the believer's *'whole armor of God'* by which our loins are to be girt, our feet are to be shod, etc. (see Ephesians 6:10–18). The admonition to *'eat it in haste'* encourages us to get all of God while we can.

> *'Seek ye the LORD **while He may be found**, call ye upon him **while He is near**.'* (Isaiah 55:6)

> *'For He will finish the work, and cut it short in righteousness: because a short work will the Lord make upon the earth.'* (Romans 9:28)

Be ready to leave!

Pass As a Guard

> *'For I will pass through the land of Egypt on that night, and will strike all the firstborn in the land of Egypt, both man and beast; and against all the gods of Egypt I will execute judgment: I am the LORD.'*
> (Exodus 12:12)

It appears from this verse that the Lord does the actual smiting upon the firstborn. Looking in verse 23, however, we see there are two different beings that will pass through the land. One who **protects**; the other who **destroys**.

> *'For the* LORD *will pass through to strike the Egyptians; and when He sees the blood on the lintel and on the two doorposts, the* LORD *will pass over the door* **and not allow (permit) the destroyer to come into your houses** *to strike you.'*   (Exodus 12:23)

Notice the Lord guards over the blood-sprinkled door and does not permit the destroyer to come in the house to smite the oldest child.

The Hebrew word for 'passover' is *pesach* and means, among other things, 'to ward off a blow' (*Wilson's Old Testament Word Studies*). In Exodus 12:23 we see that there were two separate beings who passed through the land of Egypt on that memorable midnight. The Lord was the Being who **protected** the firstborn of (Hebrew) man and beast. He is the One who 'passed as a guard' over the door of each Hebrew home in Goshen. The sole reason being obedience to God's commandment to sprinkle the lamb's blood over the upper door beam and the two side posts of each dwelling. Total obedience by each family resulted in an entire people protected with no limit of His power to work in their behalf.

The other being who **destroyed** is thought to have been the 'thief' Jesus warned us of in John 10:10 who comes *'but for to steal, and to kill and to destroy.'*

It is interesting that the word *pesach* with the same intended meaning as in Exodus 12 (according to *Wilsons'*) is used in Isaiah 31:5 (ASV) where Yahweh will defend the city of Jerusalem, it is prophesied, *'as birds hovering ... He will pass over and preserve it.'* This makes it clear that the Lord will fulfill this role as protector yet again on Israel's behalf. [2]

The Blood Token

> *'Now **the blood shall be a sign** for you on the houses where you are. And when I see the blood, I will pass over you; and the plague shall not be on you to destroy you when I strike the land of Egypt. ... And you shall take a bunch of hyssop, dip it in the blood that is in the basin, and strike the lintel and the two doorposts with the blood that is in the basin. And none of you shall go out of the door of his house until morning.'* (Exodus 12:13, 22)

If an Israelite followed the instructions to cover his doorway with the blood at the top and the sides, the Lord passed as a protector. And the plague the destroyer brought with him was not upon the Israelite house. It is interesting to note that the Egyptians were not even instructed concerning the blood covering. Pharaoh, their ruler, typifies the god of this world who has no propitiation and therefore despises those who do. Today Satan and the fallen angels have no covering in Jesus' blood.

> *'For verily He took not on Him the nature of angels; but He took on Him the seed of Abraham.'* (Hebrews 2:16)

The word 'token' means 'evidence, sign'. The blood was a sign on the houses; an evidence of divine protection. The devil could not touch that which was covered by the blood. The blood sheltered the firstborn from certain death. Without the blood, death was inevitable. Covered by the blood, protection was guaranteed. The same is true today. Our testimony of the blood overcomes the devil! (see Revelation 12:11).

Stay Under the Blood

There was one condition the blood-covered sons were obligated to keep: **they had to stay under the blood that covered them or forfeit divine protection from the destroyer!** The wording was clear:

> '... *none of you shall go out at the door of his house until the morning.*'   (Exodus 12:22)

Although we have perfect present protection from the enemy at this time, we can forfeit our claim to divine covering if we do not *'abide in Him; that when He shall appear, we may have confidence and not be ashamed before Him at His coming'* (1 John 2:28).

Many would like to think they are immune to satanic attack due to their 'hedge'. The Bible warns and informs '... *whoso breaketh an hedge, a serpent shall bite him'* (Ecclesiastes 10:8). We do have a protective hedge and covering in Jesus' blood which Satan cannot trespass. However, if we do not *'walk in the light as He is in the light'* the *'blood of Jesus Christ His Son'* does not *'cleanse us from all sin'* (see 1 John 1:7).

Our present protection can be removed by walking in any darkness at all. This reveals why holiness is a must (see Hebrews 12:14). Many years later the spies instructed Rahab to *'bind this line of scarlet thread in the window'* as the **true token** she had requested of them. The 'scarlet line' was the sign of redemption to the invading Hebrew army a few days later, and they spared Rahab and all who were in her house from destruction (see Joshua 2, 6).

The Israelites knew that scarlet was symbolic for blood (see Leviticus 14:4). Just as they had been spared in the land of Egypt by blood covering, they were to 'save alive' any who abode in the house of the harlot who had trusted by faith in the scarlet thread (see Hebrews 11:31).

The 'blood line' concept is based upon this passage in Joshua chapter two. The Israelites were blood conscious and passed this blood consciousness on to a heathen prostitute in Jericho. Today the blood of Christ is for all who come to God. All are saved from certain destruction by the blood of Jesus.

Accepting the Blood By Faith

During the time that the head of each household was applying the blood to the doorway of his home, the firstborn of the family was inside the house and remained there until morning. He was on the inside; the blood was applied to the outside door frame. He was not allowed to stick his head outside even once. This meant he could not see the blood that covered him. Neither can we see by natural sight the blood that covers us. The firstborn had to accept by faith that he was covered by the blood. We must likewise accept by faith what our Father has done for us.

Imagine the oldest son asking, 'Dad, are you sure you applied the blood just as Moses said to?' When an affirmative reply came, the son had to rely only on the integrity of his father's word. So must we. The firstborn could not see the blood nor feel the blood, but he was covered just the same.

'For we walk by faith, not by sight.'

(2 Corinthians 5:7)

Additional Notes

1. Psalm 105:37 indicates that there was not one feeble (sick or weak) person among the tribes of Israel – who made the exodus, yet later there was a law given regarding lepers (see Leviticus 13, 14, 15). Many of those who came out of Egypt strong and healthy got sick later. God established His healing covenant with Israel (Exodus 15:26) which taught if one did not walk in obedience he could be afflicted. Miriam made the exodus from Egypt and danced on the Red Sea shore (Exodus 15:20–21) and was not diseased at that time, yet later in life criticized Moses and was struck with leprosy (Numbers 12:1–15). Just because everyone was made sound the night of the passover did not mean they would always stay well. Later some became ill through rebellion, murmuring, unbelief, or disobedience, etc., and is comparable with John 5:14.

2. Satan was not working in the interest of Israel when he destroyed the firstborn of man and beast on the Passover night. Satan hates all mankind and wanted to destroy the firstborn of Israel as well as Egypt, but was prevented in doing so because the angel of the Lord stood as a guard over the blood-sprinkled doorways. Had a Hebrew family not applied the blood to the door of their home, their oldest son would have been destroyed. If it would seem contradictory that the Lord would use Satan in the accomplishment of His purposes, remember that 'The Lord hath made all things for Himself; yea, even the wicked for the day of evil' (Proverbs 16:4). When Saul rebelled against God, '...an evil spirit from the Lord troubled him' (1 Samuel 16:14). God permitted an evil spirit to trouble Saul because 'rebellion is as the sin of witchcraft' (1 Samuel 15:23). God withdrew His protective hand, and the evil spirit came in. Even in the New Testament Church in dealing with a need for church discipline, the fornicator was turned over 'to Satan for the destruction of the flesh' (1 Corinthians 5:5).

Questions on Chapter 5

1. What was the tenth and final plague brought
    upon the Egyptians? (*Hint:* It was not the
    Passover – which was the provision.)

    _____

    _____

2. Name at least three parallels between the Hebrew
    Feast of Passover and the Christian observance
    of The Lord's Supper:

    _____

    _____

    _____

    _____

3. Did darkness cover the earth during the last three
    hours of the crucifixion? Or did it cover only the
    proximity of Jerusalem?

    _____

    _____

4. Is it possible for someone who was once holy by
    the blood of Christ to later regard the blood as
    an unholy thing? If so, what judgment awaits this
    individual? (Give Scripture reference.)

    _____

    _____

    _____

5. Name at least three impurities represented by
    leaven:

    _____

    _____

6. Why did God demand that only unleavened
    bread be eaten with the Paschal (passover) lamb?

    _____

    _____

    _____

7. In what sense did Christ mean for the people to
    'eat' His flesh and 'drink' His blood?

    _____

    _____

8. Why did they roast the lamb with fire (instead of
    boiling it)?

    _____

    _____

9. Was it the Lord Himself who actually destroyed
    the firstborn of man and beast in Egypt? _____
    If not, what title is given to the being who
    performed the actual destruction? (Two words.)

    _____

10. God told the Israelites that 'the blood shall be to
    you for a **token** upon the houses' that awesome
    night. What does the word 'token' mean today?

    _____

    _____

11. Although he was covered by the blood of the passover lamb, the eldest son had to remain inside his house all night or else he would forfeit divine protection. What did the Apostle John say that would apply to this principle?

    _____

    _____

12. Could the firstborn (oldest son) see the blood that covered him? _____ How does this speak of faith in the present age of grace?

    _____

    _____

Chapter 6

Justification by the Blood
(Cleansing the Leper)

'Much more then, being now justified by His blood, we shall be saved from wrath through Him.'
(Romans 5:9)

We are justified (just-as-if-I'd never sinned) upon the basis of the blood of Christ. Justification by the blood is a new covenant truth and reality for today. The New Testament and the grace of God is **substance** whereas the Old Testament and the law of God is a **shadow**.

*'For the law having **a shadow** (outline) **of good things to come** (the new covenant)...'*
(Hebrews 10:1)

*'Which are **a shadow of things to come**; but the body is of Christ.'*
(Colossians 2:17)

This new and living way that Jesus has consecrated for us can be seen typically in the law. The law foreshadows and gives insight into the work that Christ has accomplished for us.

Leviticus 14:1–7 is only one sentence (in the KJV) and yet completely pictures the death and resurrection of our Lord Jesus Christ:

> *'And the LORD spake unto Moses, saying, This shall be the law of the leper in the day of his cleansing: He shall be brought unto the priest: And the priest shall go forth out of the camp; and the priest shall look, and, behold, if the plague of leprosy be healed in the leper; Then shall the priest command to take for him that is to be cleansed two birds alive and clean, and cedar wood, and scarlet, and hyssop: And the priest shall command that one of the birds be killed in an earthen vessel over running water: As for the living bird, he shall take it, and the cedar wood, and the scarlet, and the hyssop, and shall dip them and the living bird in the blood of the bird that was killed over the running water: And he shall sprinkle upon him that is to be cleansed from the leprosy seven times, and shall pronounce him clean, and shall let the living bird loose into the open field.'*

When God puts seven verses in one sentence, figuratively speaking, He is showing us there is one main thought in it. Many principles can be seen from this one section of Scripture but **one primary truth comes from it**.

In order to understand the spiritual truths contained in this passage, it is important to first explain the natural procedure of what happened here.

> *'Howbeit that was not first which is spiritual, but that which is natural; and afterward that which is spiritual.'*   (1 Corinthians 15:46)

First we will study the natural order of events and then proceed to discover the spiritual truth.

A leper was a man who was unclean, and due to his leprosy was put outside of fellowship with God's people – outside the camp. Wherever Israel was journeying in the wilderness they camped, and outside the main camp the excluded leper abode in a separate tent. Even though he was an Israelite, the leprosy made him unclean.

Here are some Old Testament facts about leprosy:
1. It was a sign of divine disfavor in Numbers 12:8–15.
2. It was a sign of judgment in 2 Chronicles 26:16–23.
3. It was a representation of the alienation sin produces between man and God and man and man as seen in Leviticus 13:44–46.

Thus, leprosy pictures the separation, disfavor, and judgment caused by sin. There was no cure for it among all the ancient medical remedies. It resulted in death. This compares with sin as is seen in James 1:15, *'Sin, when it is finished, bringeth forth death.'*

God provided a cleansing for the leper. No Israelite need die of this horrible disease! After confinement in a solitary dwelling for seven silent days, the victim's skin was completely healed of the disease as both Leviticus 13:46 and 14:3 teach. (Notice that God told Moses to instruct Miriam to follow these same instructions in Numbers 12:14. Miriam would not die of the disease, but evidently be healed after the seven days' isolation.)

Afterwards, the leper had to be ceremonially cleansed before coming back into the camp. The priest went outside the camp into an open field near a running stream. With him he brought two living birds that were clean according to the law. He also brought a piece of cedar wood, a small scarlet cloth, and a hyssop branch. In addition to these items, he carried an earthen vessel, or a clay pot as we say today. The head of one bird was pulled off inside this earthen vessel as it was held over the running water (stream). Then the living bird, the wood, the cloth, and the branch were dipped in the blood of the dead bird. After this the priest sprinkled blood with the hyssop branch seven times on the leper. The man was pronounced 'clean' and, finally, the living bird was released to fly into the air still wet and dripping with the former bird's blood.

Consider for a moment the great obedience that is exhibited in the Old Testament sacrifices. To the natural minds of the priests, how foolish and without meaning these and other events seemed. There was no logical reasoning or explanation for all these details. Yet without hesitation, the priests obeyed year after year the exact directions given them. They did not have the revelation of what they were doing as we have it today. Throughout the Word of God we see many instances where God instructed a person, or a people, to do certain things which to the natural mind seemed senseless. (Imagine how Peter felt when the Lord told him to get the tax money from opening a fish's mouth!)

As the liberals have, do not dismiss the details of this or any sacrifice as mere ritualism. Jesus said, *'Man shall ... live by ... every word that proceedeth out of the mouth of God'* (Matthew 4:4). Prophetically Christ speaks, *'... in the volume of the book it is written of Me'* (Psalm 40:7). Jesus is on every page of the Bible. Let's notice the spiritual truths of this beautiful passage in Leviticus.

'This shall be the law of the leper in the day of his cleansing...' It only takes a day for a leper to be

cleansed. Leprosy is a type of sin. We all were sinners. Unlike man-made religions which teach it takes many years of good works to achieve harmony with God, the Gospel teaches it only takes a day to be cleansed from our sin in the blood of Christ! (see Zechariah 3:9 and 2 Corinthians 6:2). The priest 'goes out of the camp' which shows us that our Great High Priest in making atonement for us, *'suffered without* (outside) *the gate'* (Hebrews 13:12). Jesus went outside of the gates of the city of Jerusalem in order to cleanse us. Next we come to the two birds which also symbolize Christ. He is both the priest and the birds in this passage. Why two living birds? One could be killed to symbolize the crucified Christ. The other left alive is to picture the resurrected Christ. One bird alone could not be killed and resurrected. That is the reason God commanded to take two birds. The second bird was only released after this first bird had been slain. The second bird was released in the blood of the first bird. The resurrected Christ sprinkled His own blood on the mercy-seat before the Father in heaven following His resurrection. He fulfilled the Day of Atonement work of the High Priest.

Notice the two characteristics of the birds. Alive and clean. *Alive:* Pilate testified, *'. . . nothing worthy of death is done unto Him'* (Luke 23:15). Jesus was alive and worthy of life. He had never sinned and was not worthy of sin's punishment: death. Death was totally contradictory to the nature of Jesus Christ. He **was** life (see John 14:6). *Clean: '. . . who knew no sin'* (2 Corinthians 5:21). He was separate from sin, holy and blameless. Because He was clean He had the right to remain alive.

The cedar wood symbolizes the cross. Cross in the New Testament is the word *stauros* which means 'straight pole, stake, or post set upright'. This is important because it brings forth the idea of hanging on a **tree**. [1] Cedar wood is common in the Near East. We cannot say for sure but perhaps it was on cedar wood that our Lord was nailed. Anyway, the cedar wood was dipped in the blood of the dead bird and the cross was drenched with the blood of Christ.

The scarlet was a red cloth. Scarlet pictures blood. Cloth pictures covering. '... *it is the blood that maketh an atonement* (covering) *for the soul*' (Leviticus 17:11). This scarlet cloth was red, wet with blood. Hyssop is a branch that is not very strong. It cannot support a heavy weight but was suitable for sprinkling blood.

> '*And ye shall take a bunch of hyssop, and dip it in the blood that is in the basin, and strike the lintel and the two side posts with the blood that is in the basin...*'
> (Exodus 12:22)

It was with the hyssop that the blood was transferred from the basin to the door post. The blood was applied with hyssop. Hyssop was also used to sprinkle water.

> '*And a clean person shall take hyssop, and dip it in water, and sprinkle it upon the tent...*'
> (Numbers 19:18)

Notice that a person first had to be clean before he could sprinkle water. By the sprinkling of blood a person is made clean and fit to sprinkle water. What does this water represent?

> '*Christ also loved the church, and gave Himself for it; that He might sanctify and cleanse it with the washing of water by the word...*'
> (Ephesians 5:25–26)

After we have been made clean by Christ's blood, we are in a position to be further set apart to the Father by the Word. Jesus prayed,

> *'Sanctify them through Thy truth: Thy word is truth'* (John 17:17)

Through Ezekiel God promised,

> *'Then will I sprinkle clean water upon you, and you shall be clean: from all your filthiness, and from all your idols, will I cleanse you.'* (Ezekiel 36:25)

Hyssop represents faith. It is by faith that the blood is obtained and maintained. It is by faith that we apply the Word of God to our lives.

As 'kings and priests' and as the 'royal priesthood', the believer is able to sprinkle Jesus' blood (see Revelation 1:4–6; 1 Peter 2:9). As the head of his home a father can apply the blood to his family, just as the father applied the blood to his doorposts in Exodus chapter 12. Then the head of the household can sprinkle water over his family or teach them the Word of God. Jesus demonstrated this principle when He cleansed His disciples by His spoken word.

> *'Now ye are clean through the word which I have spoken unto you.'* (John 15:3)

David prayed,

> *'Purge me with hyssop, and I shall be clean: wash me, and I shall be whiter than snow.'* (Psalm 51:7)

The earthen vessel pictures the body of humiliation that the Word (Jesus) walked in. The bird was killed **in** the earthen vessel. Jesus died in His body. Jesus gave the life of His flesh for the world. His body was created by a supernatural act of God in the womb of the virgin. However, it was a natural body like yours and mine. *Earthen* pictures clay. This speaks of a natural body made of the dust of the ground. He became actual flesh. *'We have this treasure in earthen vessels...'* (2 Cormthians 4:7). Jesus Christ is in us.

Although His body was natural, it was perfect without sin or disease. Jesus lived in perfect health. As the Word was entering earth's atmosphere, He spoke back to the Father gazing upon the womb He would shortly enter,

> *'Wherefore when He cometh into the world, He saith, Sacrifice and offering* (the blood of bulls and goats) *Thou wouldest not* (desire no more), *but **a body hast Thou prepared Me*** (to offer the perfect sacrifice with).'* (Hebrews 10:5)

> *'... we are sanctified through the offering of the **body** of Jesus Christ.'* (Hebrews 10:10)

As the Holy Spirit formed that embryo in the womb of Mary, the Word entered into it.

Earthen also means frail. In our present bodies there is no way we can experience the fullness of God's presence. We need a glorified body for that!

Now we come to the running water which was a flowing stream out in the open field. The earthen vessel was held over the running water while the first bird was killed. What does this tell us?

96

> *'How much more shall the blood of Christ, who through **the eternal Spirit** offered Himself without spot to God, purge your conscience from dead works to serve the living God?'* (Hebrews 9:14)

Running water is the shadow. 'The eternal Spirit' is the substance. Running corresponds to eternal; water is often a type of the Holy Spirit. Water is used as a symbol of the Holy Spirit more than anything else in the Scriptures. Just as the blood of the bird was shed over running water, the blood of Christ was offered through the eternal Spirit.

As the blood was shed on the cross, the Holy Spirit offered up the work of Christ before the Father. Three days later the Holy Spirit (see Romans 1:4) raised up or quickened the body and Jesus presented Himself to the Father that day (see John 20:17). The conscience is the voice of the human spirit. Our conscience is purged by the blood of Christ and the demands of righteousness are satisfied. The spirit is made alive to serve and worship the living God.

The reason the priest sprinkled the leper seven times is that seven is the Bible number for perfection or completeness. Seven is used over and over to show this. After the priest splattered him with blood, he pronounced the leper clean. What music to the leper's ears! All the days he was leprous he had to warn anyone who got near him of his condition by crying 'unclean, unclean' as he held his arm over his face in shame (see Leviticus 13:44–46). At the precise moment of the priest's pronouncement, the leper ceased to be a leper! No longer was he obligated to remain 'outside the camp' in total isolation. Now he could be reunited with his family and friends. The priest's one word: 'Clean' made all the difference!

This is a perfect picture of the judicial pronouncement from the throne of God when a sinner accepts the blood of Christ!

When we are initially cleansed by the blood, all of our sins are washed away and we are made completely clean. The Father agrees with the sacrifice of Christ, and we are pronounced clean at the very throne of God. The legal demands of sin are met and in the judicial mind of God a change in regard to us occurs. He pronounces us clean, clothes us with righteousness, and gives us eternal life. All of this occurs in the throne room.

Here on earth the Spirit bears witness to our spirit that we are a child of God. We have passed from death to life. Justification is pronounced from the throne before regeneration occurs in the human spirit. This is how one is accepted in *'the beloved'* – our Lord Jesus Christ. We are admitted into fellowship with God and His people and are no longer excluded from 'the camp'.

The living bird, dipped in the blood of the dead bird (see Revelation 19:13) is released into the open field. The bird takes wing and flies off into the sky. The resurrected Christ dipped Himself in the blood of His sacrifice and presented His blood to the Father, and *'obtained eternal redemption for us'* (Hebrews 9:12).

A SPECIAL OUTLINE

To better help the reader understand the ceremonial procedure for the cleansing of the leper and the spiritual significance it represents, I have provided the following outline.

The Leper's Cleansing Ceremony

Seven main features

1. **Two clean birds** (Jesus crucified and resurrected)
   - (a) Speaks of the crucifixion and resurrection of Jesus Christ because one bird could not be killed and then raised from the dead to fly away covered with blood.
   - (b) That both birds are types of Christ. Remember that both had to be 'alive and clean' at the beginning! (Some teach the killed bird was Christ and the living bird dipped in His blood pictures the sinner.)

2. **Cedar wood** (symbolic of the cross)
   - (a) The two birds speak of Jesus Christ.
   - (b) The cedar wood speaks of Him crucified for our sins. A crossless Christ could not have saved (see 1 Corinthians 1:18, 2:2).

3. **Scarlet** (symbolic of the atonement)
   - (a) This was a piece of red cloth. Cloth is used to cover articles and objects.
   - (b) The Hebrew word for 'atonement' (*kaphar*) means 'covering'.
   - (c) That it was scarlet in color pictures the blood of Christ shed to provide a covering for our souls.

4. **Hyssop** (a bushy plant which flourished in Palestine)
   - (a) It was used in the Old Testament to sprinkle both blood and water. See Exodus 12:22 and Numbers 19:18 for both purposes.

(b) Hyssop speaks of faith in that we apply the Blood and the Word in our lives by faith.

5. **Earthen vessel** (one bird was killed in a clay jar and all the above items were dipped in its blood in the earthen vessel)
   (a) Paul used the earthen vessel as symbolic of the natural body (2 Corinthians 4:7).
   (b) God created a body for the Word to tabernacle within as taught in Hebrews 10:5 and John 1:14.

6. **Running water** (referred to a flowing stream out in an open field where the ceremony was conducted)
   (a) The earthen vessel was held over the running water as the bird was killed.
   (b) Pictures the 'eternal Spirit' that offered the blood of Christ to the Father as seen in Hebrews 9:14.

7. **Seven times** (the priest probably used the blood-soaked hyssop with which to sprinkle the leper)
   (a) The leper was sprinkled seven times – number of perfection. This pictures the total cleansing of the heart at salvation.
   (b) Splattered with blood, the leper was told he was, at last, 'clean' – music to his ears!

Additional Notes

1. 'Tree' is translated 'timber' and is not the same Greek word as 'cross'. It is used in 1 Peter 2:24; Acts 5:30, 13:29 and Galatians 3:13. Jesus used this very word on the way to Golgotha in Luke 23:31 (see also Deuteronomy 21:22–23).

Questions on Chapter 6

1. What is our justification based upon?

_____

_____

_____

2. Why is it beneficial to study the levitical laws today?

_____

_____

_____

3. What is the one primary truth of Leviticus 14:1–7?

_____

_____

4. What does leprosy in the Old Testament picture in the New? _____ Give three scriptures in the Old Testament showing God's attitude toward leprosy and one reason why leprosy struck certain individuals.

_____

_____

_____

5. Was provision made for the physical disease of leprosy under the Law so that no Israelite need die of this horrible condition?

_____

6. Did the priests understand everything the ceremonies they performed foreshadowed in the new covenant today? _____ If not, what quality did they manifest that is desirable in our walk?

_____

_____

7. How much time did the initial cleansing ceremony require and what great truth of Christianity does it represent?

_____

_____

_____

8. What were two requirements of the sacrificial birds?

_____

_____

9. What great truth of Christianity did the two birds foreshadow?

_____

_____

10. What did the cedar wood speak of?

_____

_____

11. What did the scarlet cloth picture?

_____

_____

12. Of what new covenant reality does the hyssop speak?

_____

_____

13. Can we sprinkle the blood of Christ today?

_____

_____

14. What did the earthen vessel represent?

_____

_____

15. What does the running water speak of?

_____

_____

16. Why did the priest sprinkle the leper seven times?

_____

_____

17. What did the living bird that was released into the open field represent?

_____

_____

Chapter 7

Sanctification by the Blood
(Cleansing the Former Leper)

Our next study on the blood of Christ brings us to Leviticus 14:7. We saw in Leviticus 14:1–7 cleansing for the leper. No longer is he referred to as a leper after verse seven, for he has been pronounced clean. Yet only seven days after this pronouncement he returns to the priest for a further cleansing once more through the sprinkling of blood.

No longer are we sinners, yet further cleansing is needed. This pictures the truth that a believer is justified and pronounced clean at conversion. Desiring to be made perfect, he returns to his Great High Priest for a deeper cleansing. The seven days lapsing between the first and second cleansing pictures the desire for perfection in the heart of one whose desire is to be perfect even as His Father in heaven is perfect (see Matthew 5:48). Seven is the number of perfection.

Another benefit of our conversion experience immediately follows verse seven. In verse eight the former leper, splattered with blood, dips down into the running water under him. There in the open stream he washes himself and his clothes. This pictures the 'washing of water by the Word' cleansing for everyone who accepts the Blood. The Word cleansing follows the Blood cleansing.

In verse eight the ex-leper is allowed to leave his tent and come into the camp. No longer is he excluded as a leper from fellow Israelites. This pictures reconciliation. We are brought into *'fellowship with one another'* after we are justified (see 1 John 1:7).

On the eighth day after the leper has been pronounced clean from leprosy, he is permitted to go to the priest at the door of the tabernacle (verse 11). There he offers sacrifice to the Lord. Two he lambs and one ewe lamb without blemish are presented for a sin, trespass, and burnt offering. [1]

A log of oil is waved before the Lord for a wave offering. This brings us to the focal point of this chapter's study:

> *'And the priest shall take some of the blood of the trespass offering, and the priest shall put it upon the tip of the right ear of him that is to be cleansed, and upon the thumb of his right hand, and upon the great toe of his right foot.'* (Leviticus 14:14)

In each area, why was the blood put upon the right side of the man to be cleansed? The right side throughout the Word is **the side of divine favor**. Examples: The sheep will go on His right, the goats on His left (Matthew 25:33). Jesus is seated at the right hand of God (Mark 16:19). Jesus stretched forth His right hand and laid it upon John's shoulder (Revelation 1:17). The fishing disciples were instructed to cast the net on the right side of the ship (John 21:6). (You are never on the wrong side when you deal with the Blood. It's right!)

Remember that the Law is a shadow and the new covenant is its substance. The ear, hand, and foot in Leviticus 14:14 symbolize the believer's thought life, ministry, and fellowship. Jesus identified with us in these areas of our life.

The Passover Lamb's body was opened as a Fountain for sin (see Zechariah 13:1) in five principle areas. In the order they occurred, the Blood flowed from His back, His head, His hands, His feet, and His side. The Blood flowed from His back for our healing (1 Peter 2:24). The Blood flowed from His side to represent our position at His side in heavenly places (Ephesians 2:6) as joint-heirs (Romans 8:17). The water flowed from His side to picture His sending forth of the Holy Spirit (as we will study later) in response to His blood sacrifice.

The three places in between the back and the side were opened for our **sanctification** in the same corresponding realms of life. As the Roman soldiers forcibly plaited the crown of thorns, the Blood flowed from His head to sanctify our minds. The blood of the trespass offering was put on *the tip of the right ear of him that is to be cleansed'* symbolizing the blood of Christ sanctifying all that enters our thought life.

The blood was put on the thumb of the former leper's right hand symbolizing the blood of Christ sanctifying our works in the kingdom of God. Jesus' hands were nailed for this purpose.

The blood was put upon the Israelite's great toe that the precious Blood might be upon our walk with the Father. **Jesus' feet were nailed that ours might walk.** Unrestricted fellowship is enjoyed with the Father through the blood of the Son.

Do not let the term 'sanctification' scare you. The verb 'sanctify' means 'to set apart and to make clean'. Sanctification is the process of being separated and made clean unto God. A primary purpose of Jesus' suffering for us was to accomplish this cleansing aspect in the lives of His people.

> *'Wherefore Jesus also,* **that He might sanctify the people with His own blood,** *suffered without* (outside) *the gate.'* (Hebrews 13:12)

Jesus is the Sanctifier, the people are the object of His sanctifying grace, the Blood is the means of cleansing, or the sanctifying agent. Or, Jesus is **the One who makes men holy with His own blood.**

> *'For both He that sanctifieth and they who are sanctified are all of one...'* (Hebrews 2:11)

The Thought Life

The first area of cleansing for the former leper is the ear. **We need the Blood on what we hear.** How well David knew the distracting voice of the enemy!

> *'I am restless in my complaint and am surely distracted because of the voice of the enemy...'*
> (Psalm 55:2–3, NASB)

Many are distracted from spiritual devotion due to satanic interference. Others find their minds assaulted by an obsession of demonized thoughts. The blood of Christ provides the legal basis for victory in the believer's thought life.

As our Great Substitute, the Man who never had an evil thought (although He did have thoughts of evil) transferred His pure mind to us by His blood.[2] *'We have the mind of Christ,'* and freedom from slavery to sin in our thoughts (1 Corinthians 2:16). Our ear is set apart to God picturing that the disciple can hear his Master's voice. Our Substitute took all our wicked imaginations when He was offered in our place to God. He never had mental wickedness, yet He took ours in the crown of thorns in order to provide mental purity for us.

For thirty-three years Jesus walked in a natural body and was subject to all the temptations we are. Satan attempted to flash vile pictures across His thought processes. Not once did Jesus entertain and give place to a thought from the evil one.

On the other hand, the sinner harbored evil imaginations and toyed with vile thoughts from an early age.

Jesus was never polluted in His mind and by the amazing wonder of the Substitution Principle provided a holy mind for all who believe. He puts the Blood on our mind in a similar manner that the levitical priest put the blood on the tip of the right ear. Our mind is separated unto God and made a holy receptacle of His Word. When our thoughts are fixed on Him, we have perfect peace on the basis of His blood.

You can silence the voice of the accuser by openly testifying the merits of Jesus' blood.

> '*And they overcame him* (the accuser) *by the blood of the Lamb, and by the word of their testimony* (vocal agreement); *and they loved not their lives unto the death* (their wills were fully fixed on the Father's will).'   (Revelation 12:11)

All the divine revelation and illumination the Christian receives comes from the Holy Spirit through the Word on the legal ground of the Blood. As a priest in the kingdom of God, you are privileged to sprinkle with His blood. The phrase 'plead the blood of Jesus' is not actually in the Bible, but a like principle is taught throughout. Different individuals sprinkled the blood upon both people and places (see Exodus 12:22–23, 24:6–8, 29:16–21; Leviticus 3:1–8; Hebrews 9:21).

All the Christian's material possessions are legally under the protection of the Blood. The firstborn of the beast did not die if the owner sprinkled the blood upon the door of his home (see Exodus 12). The blood of Jesus is a weapon of our warfare, but we must use it daily to enjoy the benefits derived therefrom.

The Believer's Works

Next, the blood was applied to the thumb of the right hand. The hand pictures one's works in the Word of God. Consider the following scriptures:

The Ministry of the Word

'And Jesus said unto him, No man, having put **his hand to the plough**, and looking back, is fit for the kingdom of God.'   (Luke 9:62)

The Healing Ministry

'And these signs shall follow them that believe; In My name ... they shall **lay hands on the sick**, and they shall recover.'   (Mark 16:17–18)

The Believer's Works

'Whatsoever **thy hand findeth to do**, do it with thy might...'   (Ecclesiastes 9:10)

> *'And let the beauty of the LORD our God be upon us:
> and establish Thou **the works of our hands** upon us;
> yea, the work of our hands establish thou it.'*
>
> (Psalm 90:17)

The Believer's Warfare

> *'**Blessed** be the LORD my strength, which teacheth
> my hands to war, and my fingers to fight.'*
>
> (Psalm 144:1)

> *'Let the high praises of God be in their mouth, and a
> two-edged sword in their hand.'*   (Psalm 149:6)

In these passages hands can be compared to works. Our works in the Church are the same as our particular ministries in the Body of Christ. Sowing and reaping are both operations effected by the hand in actual farming. Sowing the Word and reaping the harvest are the mission of the believer (cf. Psalm 126:6). Our ministry is effective with the Blood sprinkled upon it, and ineffectual apart from the Blood. Unconfessed sin allows Satan to bind our hands to keep one's ministry from functioning properly.

Consider your works prior to salvation. Your hands framed wickedness and worked deceit. Consider Jesus' hands. For thirty-three years He did nothing wrong at all; His works were all holy. [3] The first thirty years His hands were employed in the art of carpentry. He made beautiful objects from raw materials. He built tables, chairs, and other needful articles. He never stole or destroyed another's property. After the wilderness experience He returned to Galilee in the power of the Spirit laying hands on the sick, breaking and multiplying bread and fish, raising fallen people, and doing good. His hands did not deserve the nails, but by the blood that flowed from His hands ours are now clean from their former filth and set apart for the work of God.

Every good deed performed by the Christian is acceptable to God as a pleasing sacrifice only through the blood of Christ. When we lay our hands on the sick, the devil flees. Before conversion I committed many acts of sin by which Satan employed my hands for advancement of darkness. Today these very hands are used by God. It is all by the sanctifying grace afforded in Jesus and His blood. *'Blessed be the LORD my strength, **which teacheth my hands to war, and my fingers to fight'*** (Psalm 144:1).

When the enemy begins to interfere with your works and ministry, overcome his binding attacks by confessing the merits of the blood against him (see James 4:7). As a member of the royal priesthood, you can sprinkle the blood on your ministry.

Our Walk With God

The third place the blood was applied to him that was to be cleansed was upon the great (big) toe of his right foot. This corresponds to the area of fellowship with God. Notice the connection between walking and fellowship:

> *'But if we walk in the light, as He is in the light, we have fellowship one with another, and the blood of Jesus Christ His Son cleanseth* (and keeps on cleansing) *us from all sin.'*   (1 John 1:7)

If we walk with God we have fellowship. There are several instances in the Scriptures where a man 'walked with God' as meaning his fellowship with Him (see

111

Genesis 3:8, 5:22, 6:9, 13:17–18). The blood of Jesus Christ provides a basis for continual fellowship by continual cleansing. God is of purer eyes than to behold evil and cannot look with favor on iniquity (see Habakkuk 1:13).

Although we were initially cleansed at salvation, further cleansing is needed as the years go by because God cannot fellowship with us when sin is present in our lives. Sometimes all of us miss the mark and must confess our sin that the blood may be applied. Without confession of sin there is no application of the blood (see 1 John 1:9). God's ideal for us is *'that ye sin not'* (1 John 2:1–2), but has made adequate provision for uncleanness in the Christian's life in the meritorious sacrifice of Christ. As we mentioned in the last chapter, Jesus is not only the Sin Offering for our initial redemption but is the Trespass Offering for our sanctification as well.

The most enjoyable aspect of the new life is fellowship with God. Our feet may stay in step with God when set apart by the Blood that we may get to know the Father intimately.

The Oil On the Blood

This study would not be complete without Leviticus 14:17. Immediately after verse 14, the topic turns from the blood to oil:

> *'And the priest shall take some of the log of oil, and pour it into the palm of his own left hand. Then the priest shall dip his right finger in the oil that is in his left hand, and shall sprinkle some of the oil with his finger seven times before the LORD. And of the rest of the oil in his hand, the priest shall put some on the*

> *tip of the right ear of him who is to be cleansed, on
> the thumb of his right hand, and on the big toe of his
> right foot, on the blood of the trespass offering.'*
> (Leviticus 14:15–17)

It goes without saying that oil is a type of the anointing of the Holy Spirit. All students of the Word agree at this point. The oil was sprinkled seven times before the Lord, showing that the Spirit proceeds to us from the Father. Jesus verbalized this truth in John 15:26,

> *'But when the Comforter is come whom I will send
> unto you from the Father, even the Spirit of truth,
> which proceedeth from the Father, He shall testify
> of Me.'*

The rest of the oil in the priest's hand was put in the same spot on the man that the blood had been put only a few moments previously. The Lord instructed, *'... put the oil ... upon the blood ...'* Put the oil on the blood. Where the blood was not, the oil was not. The priest anointed the Israelite with oil only after he was touched by blood. It is true today that the Lord anoints us with fresh oil of the Holy Spirit only after we are covered by the blood of Christ. If we honor the blood, God will honor us with the Holy Spirit working on our behalf. The thought life is inspired as the oil is put on the ear. Our ministry is empowered afresh as the Holy Spirit quickens. Our fellowship with God is enriched as the Comforter communicates between the Father and His children. We hear God's voice, work the works of God, and walk with the Father as the Spirit enables. Charles Wesley showed this understanding of the oil after the blood when he sang, 'The Spirit answers to the Blood.' When there is a lack of anointing, examine

113

yourself in regard to the Blood. **The Blood is the legal basis of authority; the Holy Spirit gives the actual empowering.**

The Full Anointing

After the Israelite was anointed in the three specific areas, the oil was poured all over his head and coursed down his garments.

> *'And the remnant of the oil that is in the priest's hand he shall pour upon the head of him that is to be cleansed: and the priest shall make an atonement for him before the LORD.'* (Leviticus 14:18)

This represents the fullness of the Spirit upon the believer. All he does is anointed with the Holy Spirit. How beautiful it would be to walk in this measure of the overall anointing! (This compares to Aaron's anointing in Psalm 133:2.)

OUTLINE OF LEVITICUS 14:1–18

In the last two chapters we have covered most of Leviticus 14:1–18 verse by verse. To enhance your overall view I have diagrammed the passage below containing some additional insights not previously included. Jesus Himself referred to the law concerning the cleansing of the leper in Matthew 8:1–4, when after He had healed a leper instructed him to go 'to the priest and offer the gift that Moses commanded, for a testimony unto them' that his skin had been healed.

Subject: The Cleansing of the Leper

NT Parallel: How God changes a sinner into a saint

I. The initial cleansing (Leviticus 14:1–7)

NT Truth: Justification by the Blood (Romans 5:9)

1. After leprosy had been clearly diagnosed by a levitical priest, according to the specifications of Leviticus 13:2–59, the infected person was pronounced unclean and shut up in an isolated dwelling (tent) for seven full days. If anyone came near him he had to cry 'unclean, unclean' giving the person full warning of his condition. Family and friends were put far from him.

   (a) If the leper looked to Yahweh-Rapha during this bleak period of solitude, healing was virtually guaranteed as promised in God's healing covenant in Exodus 15:26.

   (b) Unlike all the other primitive peoples who were literally sentenced to a slow and agonizing death if they contracted leprosy, the Hebrew need not fear such a fate, if he would go according to God's laws.

2. After the leprosy had been healed by God's power, the priest would inspect him to make sure the skin was clear. In order to inspect him, the priest 'went out of the camp' much like our Lord Jesus 'suffered without the gate' in order to cleanse us with His blood (Hebrews 13:12).

3. The ceremonial cleansing, which is the teaching of this text, only-required one day's time. At the conclusion of the ceremony, the leper was pronounced clean (Leviticus 14:7) and nevermore called a leper in the entire passage (through Leviticus 14:20).

4. There are seven items which figure into the cleansing ceremony:
   (a) Two clean birds
   (b) Cedar wood
   (c) Scarlet (cloth)
   (d) Hyssop (branch)
   (e) Earthen vessel
   (f) Running water (stream)
   (g) Sprinkled seven times

5. One of the birds was killed (by pulling off its head) and its blood was poured into the earthen vessel (clay jar). Then the living bird, the cedar wood, the scarlet cloth, and the hyssop branch were all dipped in the blood of the slain bird in the earthen vessel. Both priest and leper were standing in a stream. One of them held the vessel while the other killed the bird and dipped the other bird and the other items in its blood.

6. The priest then splattered the leper (by using the blood-soaked hyssop branch) a total of seven times. When he was thus covered and wet with blood the priest told him he was finally **clean!** (God sees us clean when the blood of Christ covers us.) **Justification** is a legal pronouncement from the throne of God; **regeneration** is an actual experience in the heart of man. The legal pronouncement occurs only at the precise moment that a sinner sincerely calls on the Lord Jesus. The Holy Spirit bears witness to the pronouncement in heaven and gives birth to a new spirit within the person.

7. The living bird was released 'into the open field' which may signify the difficulty it had trying to fly (as it was drenched wet with blood). Soon, however, it was able to take wing and fly off never again to be seen by the priest or the former leper. How little

could either realize the tremendous significance of the two birds – a picture of both the death and resurrection of Jesus, who carried the blood of His cross into the heavenly temple! As our High Priest, He sprinkled the blood of His sacrifice upon the mercy-seat (the throne of God). But the natural ceremony has it limitations – we will see our Redeemer because He will return again.

(a) Some have taught the two birds typify the Lord Jesus (who was killed) and the sinner (who is dipped in His blood in order to fly into heaven). We disagree with this view (although we recognize merit in it), because the birds had to be **alive** and **clean** at the beginning of the ceremony.

(b) The sinner is dead in sins and trespasses wearing the filthy rags of his spiritual graveclothes (see Ephesians 2:1; Isaiah 64:6).

8. This initial cleansing ceremony beautifully typifies Romans 5:9. It pictures the evangelical truth of **justification**.

II. *Home at last!* (Leviticus 14:8–9)

NT Truth: Reconciliation (Ephesians 2:12–20)

1. With the isolation now behind him, the former leper could now be restored to family and friends. But first, what to do about the blood splattered on his clothes and on his person? After the priest pronounced him 'clean' the man dipped into the water he had been standing in throughout the ceremony and washed off himself and his clothes.

(a) This typifies *'the washing of water by the Word'* (Ephesians 5:26), which is so vital after conversion. A new convert needs to soak in the Scriptures learning them on a surface understanding level. This provides a good foundation the Lord can build upon.

(b) The water bath was accompanied with the removal of body hair – ouch! – *'put off the old man'* (Ephesians 4:22–24).

2. After he had thoroughly washed and shaved his new, healed skin, he was ready to be seen and hugged by his loved ones. *'And after that he shall come into the camp.'* What joy at this reunion! We are no more strangers and foreigners – but fellow citizens with the saints of all the ages! (see Ephesians 2:19–20).

3. Seven days later, however, he had to shave off all his hair once more. He also had to thoroughly wash himself and his clothes again.

III. *Cleaned a second time* (Leviticus 14:10–14)

NT Truth: Sanctification by the blood (Hebrews 13:12)

1. The eighth day following the initial pronouncement of cleanness found the same Israelite before the priest again – for another cleansing! He had been pronounced clean already and was no longer regarded as a leper. Yet, he still needed the blood applied once more. What rich symbolism of the fact that we are no longer regarded sinners, yet we still need further cleansing in our walk with God.

2. Two male lambs were brought for sacrifice. Both male lambs picture the Lord Jesus even as both clean birds had spoken of Him the week earlier. In Bible typology two of the same speak of two aspects of the one. In this instance the two 'he lambs' picture Jesus as both Savior and Sanctifier.

(a) One lamb was offered as a *'sin offering'* (Leviticus 14:19). In the literal Hebrew the word is *c'hatt* and is used of Jesus in 2 Corinthians 5:21

('made sin for us') in the Hebrew Bible. The *c'hatt* was 'most holy' and was killed *'in the holy place'* (Leviticus 14:13). The Sin Offering pictures **Jesus the Savior** who redeemed and justified us by His blood (Romans 5:9; Revelation 5:9–10). Zechariah foresaw a Fountain opened *'for sin'* (salvation) and *'for uncleanness'* (sanctification).

(b) The other lamb was killed for *'a trespass offering'* (Leviticus 14:12–13). It is *'asham* in Hebrew. It was killed first – before the sin offering was killed. The reason for this is clearly seen, inasmuch as Jesus poured out His blood for our sanctification (the head, hands, and feet), before He poured out His blood for our justification (the side). The *'asham* is ascribed to Messiah in Isaiah 53:10 where it is incorrectly translated *'an offering for sin'* rather than *'an offering for trespass'* or *'a trespass offering'*. The Trespass Offering pictures **Jesus the Sanctifier** who makes us holy with His blood (Hebrews 13:12).

3. The 'ewe lamb' is a picture of the Bride of Christ. Notice, she is not offered for sin or for trespass, but only *'for a burnt offering'* (Leviticus 14:13, 19). She is killed, like the other two lambs, in the holy place, and after the sin offering is slain. This pictures the Church's personal sacrifice to God which is a sweet-smelling savor unto Him (see Romans 12:1; Galatians 2:20). She is killed following the death of the sin offering picturing our consecration follows that of Christ's personal sacrifice and in identification with His (*'I am crucified with Christ...'*). She is offered with the 'meat (literally meal) offering' which consisted of 'three tenth deals' (or one peck)

119

of 'fine flour' (symbolizing purity. The truth of the burnt offering is that whereas Jesus was offered for our salvation and to make us holy before God, we must offer ourselves as living sacrifices.

  (a) Paul said, *'For I am now ready to be offered* (lit., sacrificed)... ' (2 Timothy 4:6).

  (b) He also said, *'Yea, and if I be offered* (or, poured forth as an oblation) *upon the sacrifice and service of your faith, I joy, and rejoice with you all'* (Philippians 2:17).

4. The blood of the trespass offering was put on three spots on the Israelite: the right ear, the right thumb, and the big toe of the right foot.

  (a) In each case it was applied to the right side, picturing divine favor.

  (b) Each anatomical place corresponds to a working of grace in the believer today, i.e., the thought life, the works, and the walk.

5. In Exodus 29:20 the exact same procedure was followed in the consecration of priests to the priest's office. This is the priesthood cleansing all new covenant priests must experience before their priestly ministry can be pleasing to the Lord.

IV. *Anointed with oil* (Leviticus 14:14–18)

NT Truth: The anointing of the Spirit (1 John 2:20–27)

1. The subject abruptly shifts from the trespass lamb to the log of oil. It was waved before the Lord before the lamb was killed thus consecrating it for divine service (Leviticus 14:12). The priest opens the log (bottle) of oil and pours some into the palm of his own left hand (Leviticus 14:15). He then dips his right forefinger in the oil and sprinkles it seven times before the Lord (toward the Holy of Holies (Leviticus 14:16)). This signifies that the anointings of

God can only come from Him and go back to Him. He never gives an anointing for our personal magnification, but only for the accomplishment of His purpose which brings Him glory (see John 14:16, 26).

2. The priest then took his forefinger once more and dipped it in the oil in his left palm. This time he carefully applied the oil to the tip of the right ear, the thumb of the right hand, and the great toe of the right foot of the Israelite. Moses specifically instructed *'put the oil ... upon the blood'* (Leviticus 14:17). Where there was no blood there was to be no oil (until the following verse where the remainder of the oil was poured over his head).

   (a) The oil on the ear signifies the Holy Spirit speaking to us (Revelation 2:7, 11, 17, 29, 3:6, 13, 22).

   (b) The oil on the thumb signifies the anointing of the Holy Spirit upon our ministries (Acts 1:8, 10:38). [This is beautifully typed in Genesis 8:11 – the dove brought an olive leaf to Noah after he put forth his hand and took her. The Holy Spirit is **not** the anointing, but the Holy Spirit **gives** the anointing(s).]

   (c) The oil on the toe signifies walking in the Spirit (Galatians 5:16). The power of the Holy Spirit is available to us in our earthly walk and our everyday life.

3. The remnant of the oil in the bottle is poured upon the head of the Israelite. The first high priest of Israel, Aaron, was the first anointed this way (Psalm 133:2), just as our High Priest had *'the Spirit without measure'* (John 3:34).

   (a) Some have a problem with this aspect since God previously commanded: *'Upon man's flesh* shall it not be poured' (Exodus 30:32). This obviously referred to a natural use of the holy anointing oil. The cleansing of the former leper was a holy use, just like the anointing on the priesthood (Exodus 30:30).

(b) A careful study of Exodus 30:22–33 reveals how sacred God views the precious anointing of the Holy Spirit.

4. The anointing oil on the former leper (common Israelite) and on the priesthood corresponds to the new covenant believer in both respects. The believer is a former sinner, made righteous by faith in Jesus' sacrifice, and is a priest unto God as well (1 Peter 2:5, 9; Revelation 1:5, 6, 5:9, 10).

V. Additional facts about leprosy

1. The laws for determining what was leprosy (as opposed to a skin rash) were given to the priesthood in Leviticus 13. If a man was determined to be leprous, he was to be shut up for seven days, during which it is implied, he would be healed. If not, he was shut up seven days more. During this period of darkness and isolation the Israelite would focus all this thoughts upon Yahweh and call out to Him to fulfill His role of Yahweh-Rapha (Exodus 15:26).

2. Leprosy was a sign of divine disfavor (as in the case of Miriam (Numbers 12:1–15)) and even divine judgment (as in the case of Uzziah (2 Chronicles 26:16–23)) whenever God's covenant people, Israel, contracted it. They were considered 'unclean' and 'defiled' spiritually as well as physically (hence, the shedding of blood in Leviticus 14).

3. Leprosy, it is historically documented, was universally feared in all ancient societies and especially prevalent in Egypt (even with all their physicians).

It is perhaps referred to in Deuteronomy 28:27 as *'the itch whereof thou canst not be healed'* and/or as *'a sore botch that cannot be healed, from the sole of thy foot unto the top of thy head'* (Deuteronomy 28:35). There was no known cure for this dreaded and painful disease that literally ate up the skin by chunks. God, who had established Himself as Israel's physician at the waters of Marah, was the only One who could remedy this fatal condition. Israel had covenant rights for healing (although many apostatized from this revelation after Solomon imported physicians with his wives and idols). Yahweh made provision for the healing of this disease as must be agreed by every honest heart who studies Leviticus 13 and 14. It is obvious that the leprous condition would be short term (only one week from the unclean pronouncement to the clean pronouncement – compare Leviticus 13:44 with 14:7). Otherwise it was certain to be a long and agonizing death. Note the lepers at the gate of Samaria who honestly appraised their condition: *'Why sit we here until we die?'* (2 Kings 7:3). Yahweh proved Himself the conqueror of leprosy many, many times throughout Israel's history. Naaman, a Syrian who had no covenant rights with Israel's God, received a mercy healing in 2 Kings 5.

4. Leprosy is the most graphic type of **sin** in the Old Testament. Sin isolates (Isaiah 59:1–2); defiles (Isaiah 64:6); and kills (James 1:15). Jesus (Yahshua) is the only One who can remedy this horrible condition that afflicts all of mankind (Matthew 1:21).

This account of the cleansing of the leper is indeed marvelous, for we see the transforming grace of God.

From condemned in leprosy to exaltation in God's anointings, the former sinner is transformed into a saint.

Additional Notes

1. The blood of *the sin offering* (*c'hatt*) is not applied to the former leper since he was pronounced clean one week earlier. The blood of **the trespass offering** (*'asham*) is now applied. As Christians, we have already been cleansed through the Lamb's blood as our sin offering. Now we need His blood for our trespasses.

2. Our Lord Jesus Christ never had an evil thought. He was 'undefiled' (Hebrews 7:26) and He said, 'Evil thoughts ... defile the man' (see Mark 7:20–23). **Had He had one evil thought, He would have been defiled.** This is not to say He had no thought of or from (the) evil (one). The difference is that an evil thought 'comes from within', while a thought of evil comes from an outside source (the tempter). A thought of evil turns into an evil thought if the will accepts what has come from without. Jesus' will always delighted in doing the will of God; thus the thoughts of the evil one were repelled. Jesus was tempted in His thoughts, it is true, but never yielded in His mind.

3. Contrary to popular opinion, the Scriptures do not say that Christ struck the money changers with the scourge of small cords when He drove them out of the temple (see Matthew 21:12–14; Mark 11:14–19; Luke 19:44–48; John 2:14–17).

Questions on Chapter 7

1. Whereas Leviticus 14:1–7 primarily foreshadow the work of justification, what do verses 14–18 primarily represent?

   _____

   _____

2. What do the seven days lapsing between the first and second cleansings represent?

   _____

   _____

   _____

3. After the leper is pronounced clean, he is permitted to leave his solitary tent and come back into the camp. What does this picture?

   _____

   _____

4. After the sprinkling of blood upon the Hebrew, he is instructed to wash himself in water. What does this speak of in our experience today?

   _____

   _____

5. On the eighth day following his initial cleansing, what does the former leper do?

   _____

   _____

   _____

6. What does the priest do with the blood of **the trespass offering**?

   _____

   _____

   _____

   _____

7. Why was the blood applied to the right rather than the left side of the Hebrew?

   _____

   _____

   Give at least two Scriptures which speak of the significance of the right side:

   _____

   _____

8. What were the five principal areas of the body of the Lamb of God that were opened for us?

   (a) _____

   (b) _____

   (c) _____

   (d) _____

   (e) _____

9. What does each of the five above areas correspond to in the believer's life today?

   (a) _____

   (b) _____

(c) _____

(d) _____

(e) _____

10. Did Jesus ever have an evil thought? Why?

_____

_____

_____

11. How can one silence the voice of the accuser?

_____

_____

12. Is it proper for believers to claim divine help for the thought life? _____ On what basis?

_____

_____

_____

13. Name at least four specific functions represented by **the hands** in Scripture:

(a) _____

(b) _____

(c) _____

(d) _____

14. What does the application of the blood to the foot signify?

_____

_____

15. What does the oil represent? Why was it applied only after the blood had been applied?

_____

_____

_____

_____

16. Can you chart your spiritual progress according to the outline of Leviticus 14:1–18?

_____

What verse have you attained to by the grace of God?

_____

_____

Chapter 8

The Open Fountain

Jesus Christ is the focal object and central theme of the Word of God for He is the Word Himself (see Revelation 19:13). The One of whom the prophets spoke is none other than our Lord. There has never been another individual who fulfilled biblical prophecy so perfectly and completely.

Zechariah foresaw a fountain flowing which provided cleansing for sin and for uncleanness:

> 'In that day there shall be a fountain opened to the house of David and to the inhabitants of Jerusalem for sin and for uncleanness.' (Zechariah 13:1)

In That Day

Messianic prophecy often refers to a special period of time. Jesus referred to that day as His hour. At the onset of His ministry He stated, *'Mine hour is not yet come'* (John 2:4). Sometime later in ministering to His disciples, He answered them saying, *'The hour is come, that the Son of man should be glorified'* (John 12:23).

In contemplating this hour He admitted,

> *'Now is My soul troubled; and what shall I say?*
> *Father, save Me from this hour: But for this cause*
> *came I unto this hour. Father, glorify Thy name.*
> *Then came there a voice from heaven saying, I have*
> *both glorified it, and will glorify it again.'*
>
> (John 12:27–28)

The day of which Zechariah spoke about a fountain being opened was the hour the Son of Man was crucified. For the Lord of hosts had promised, *'I will remove the iniquity of that land in one day'* (Zechariah 3:9). In a short day's time the Lamb of God became the sin offering for the whole world.

We are living in that same day referred to by Paul as *'the day of salvation ... now is the acceptable time'* (2 Corinthians 6:2). The day Zechariah spoke of began when Jesus was nailed to the tree, and will continue right up to Armageddon. All the nations that come against Jerusalem will be divinely destroyed. The house of David and the inhabitants of Jerusalem will look upon their Deliverer from heaven whom their race previously pierced They will ask,

> *'What are these wounds in Thine hands? Then He*
> *shall answer, Those with which I was wounded in the*
> *house of My friends.'*
>
> (Zechariah 13:6; see also 12:9–14)

They will realize the mistake their forefathers made many centuries ago and will accept Jesus as their Messiah. *'And so all Israel shall be saved ... '* (Romans 11:26).

Jesus Christ was a fountain sealed until the day His skin was pierced. **When the skin of His body was**

130

punctured, the fountain was opened. He is the source of the cleansing stream that washes away our sins.

> *'Unto Him that loved us, and washed us from our sins in His own blood.'* (Revelation 1:5)

God's Predetermined Plan

The Roman soldiers were not following their own plan of execution. They unknowingly followed a foreseen, foreknown, and fore-fixed plan devised much earlier: before the world was even made. Redemption was planned before creation was performed!

Peter caught a glimpse of the predetermined plan. In the first sermon preached in the day of salvation he stated,

> *'Him, being delivered by the determinate counsel* (predetermined plan) *and foreknowledge of God, ye have taken, and by wicked hands have crucified and slain.'* (Acts 2:23)

Jesus Christ was crucified according to a predetermined plan in the mind of God. This *'determinate counsel'* was the Godhead taking counsel with each other prior to the creation (see also Acts 15:18; Hebrews 4:3).

Adam's sin did not catch God off guard. The Father foresees and foreknows. The exact manner in which Jesus would become the sin offering was laid out in eternity. In the Revelation, John also saw, *'... the Lamb slain from the foundation of the world...'* (Revelation 13:8). **The exact procedure to the very detail was foreknown.** To this the prophets agree. It was foreseen in the Spirit that Christ would be spit upon and His beard plucked (see Isaiah 50:6). It was predetermined that His appearance would be marred (see Isaiah 52:14).

It was foreknown that He would be smitten, pierced through, bruised, whipped, scourged, despised, oppressed, afflicted, and numbered with the criminals (see Isaiah 53). The Word pre-incarnate spoke through David, *'They have pierced My hands and My feet'* (Psalm 22:16). Even in Deuteronomy the curse was put on those hung on a tree, foreshadowing the curse Jesus would bear (see Deuteronomy 21:23; Galatians 3:13). Jesus foretold His own crucifixion saying,

> *'And I, if I be lifted up from the earth, will draw all men unto Me. This He said, signifying what* (manner of) *death He should die.'* (John 12:32–33)

In this light the Holy Spirit revealed the manner and procedure in which the Fountain was opened, and its great importance to the child of God.

The order in which the five principal areas of His body were opened is of primary importance. We just studied the three in-between areas (head, hands, feet) in the previous chapter, considering their spiritual importance. We study in chapter 12 the spiritual importance of the fifth area being opened – His side – and will see why the water flowed. Now, however, we will focus our attention to the mechanical aspects of the crucifixion, or the physical aspects of Jesus' sacrifice: how the Fountain was opened.

The Roman Scourge

The **back** was opened with a Roman scourge outside Pilate's Judgment Hall at the whipping post. Jesus had been awake at least 24 hours at this time and was physically worn, as well as emotionally exhausted. The wonder that He survived the Roman scourge is remarkable. It goes to prove that no man could take His life from Him (see John 10:18).

The Roman scourge (Latin: *flagellum*) was far different from the commonly thought of cat-of-nine-tails which was developed centuries later. As all Roman weapons, the flagellum, was precision-built and masterfully employed. The sharp bronze metal tips pierced at equally distant points into Jesus' back. The blows were placed high on the shoulder area and ripped the flesh in straight lines to the buttocks area. Christ foretold this experience in the Psalms comparing His scourging to the plowing of a field.

> *'The plowers plowed upon My back: they made long their furrows.'* (Psalm 129:3)

The plowers were the Roman soldiers. They plowed with the Roman scourge. They made long the stripes from the top to the bottom of His back. Again He speaks centuries before He was tied to the whipping post.

> *'I gave My back to the smiters...'* (Isaiah 50:6)

It is commonly thought that 39 blows were inflicted upon Him due to the Jewish custom of that time. However, Jesus was scourged by the Romans and not by the Jews. According to all sources I have studied, He may have been beaten more than Jewish custom or less depending upon the whim of the soldiers. The blood gushed from His back. The Father gave the Son strength to accomplish the predetermined plan. The mind of Deity fore-planned the whipping post as the means by which the sicknesses and pains of many would be borne. It must have seemed most peculiar to the soldiers that this Fellow did not resist them as they led Him from the Judgment Hall to the whipping post. It is well known that an average of four soldiers would drag the criminal to the post. Christ *'gave* (His) *back to the smiters.'* What a Savior! He knew that by so doing Isaiah's prophecy *'and with His stripes we are healed'* would be fulfilled. The stripes, of course, were red stripes: the blood that flowed from His back purchased our healing.

The Crown of Thorns

The crown of thorns woven from the common thorn-bush in the Middle East opened Jesus' **head** to let the cleansing stream flow. Different from most thorn-bushes in North America, this bush had smaller thorns but many more of them. A sharply stinging poison resident in the thorn was released into His scalp as the mock crown was platted on His head and smitten with the reed (see Matthew 27:29–30). This stinging sensation caused a tormenting itch and burning. This pictures the poisonous thoughts the wicked have imagined.

The blood flowed soaking this mock crown, showing the protection we have today from evil spirits. It is widely known that the rattlesnake and the roadrunner are common enemies. One way the desert birds fight the rattlesnake is head on. Another way is that the chapparal birds, or roadrunners, assemble prickly cactus leaves surrounding a sleeping rattler. When it awakens from its afternoon siesta, it finds itself imprisoned by the cactus needles. Unable to cross over the prickly barrier and fully frustrated, the fangs are thrust into its own body and death shortly transpires.

We have a protective hedge for our minds in the blood of Christ. The crown of thorns soaked with blood afforded the provision of *'the helmet of salvation'* (Ephesians 6:17). If we keep our helmet on, there can be no invasion of the enemy into our minds. Just as the smart chapparal birds prepare a barrier for the snake, the Christian must make a sure defense for his thought life on the legal basis of the blood. If we do not break our hedge protection, the serpent cannot corrupt our minds (compare Ecclesiastes 10:8 with 2 Corinthians 11:2–3).

The Spikes and the Spear

The last three areas of Jesus' body, our Fountain, were opened on the cross. **His hands** were nailed by the sharp Roman spikes into the wood. We have a certain idea that His hands were nailed directly over His head since the cross was most likely a tree post set upright. This would increase pressure causing the lungs to collapse more quickly than if they were nailed to a horizontal cross beam. [1] The Greek word for hands includes the wrist area. It was probably through the middle of the wrists between the bones that the nails were driven. This would aid in holding the body on the cross since the nails would have torn through the palm area under the weight of His body.

His feet were placed the one over the other while the spike was driven into His flesh. He was nailed to the cross while the timber pole was on the ground. No doubt several soldiers heaved the pole with the Sacrifice into the air. *'... they pierced My hands and My feet'* (Psalm 22:16).

It was the custom of the soldiers to break the legs of those still living toward late afternoon to hasten death.

> *'But when they came to Jesus and saw that He was already dead, they did not break His legs. But one of soldiers pierced His side with a spear, and immediately blood and water came out.'* (John 19:33–34)

This fulfilled the Scriptures once more for David said, *'He keeps all His bones: not one of them is broken'* (Psalm 34:20). Concerning the Passover Lamb we read:

> *'Neither shall ye break a bone thereof.'*
> (Exodus 12:46)

Later Paul tells us,

> *'Christ our Passover* (lamb) *is sacrificed for us.'*
> (1 Corinthians 5:7)

The Messiah's skeleton, unlike the others crucified that day, remained whole.

Additional Notes

1. There is no need for controversy on this relatively lesser issue. The word for 'cross' is *stauros* and is defined as 'a pole or post set upright'. Perhaps the bark was still on it lending to the other term, 'tree', which appears rather often after the Gospels (see Acts 5:30, Galatians 3:13, 1 Peter 2:24). Our modern cross came to wide use in recent centuries.

Questions on Chapter 8

1. Who is the focal object and central theme of the
    Word of God and why?

    _____

    _____

2. What did Zechariah foresee concerning the
    sacrifice of Christ (what metaphor did he use of
    Him)?

    _____

    _____

    _____

3. According to Zechariah, how long would it take
    God to remove the sin of the land?

    _____

4. How was it that Jesus became 'a fountain opened
    for sin'?

    _____

    _____

    _____

5. Were the Roman soldiers limited to the Jewish
    custom of forty stripes save one (39 blows)?

    _____

    What reference in Isaiah predicted that our Savior
    would offer no resistance to the Roman soldiers
    who whipped Him?

    _____

6. Why did the Roman soldiers not break the legs of Christ?

_____

_____

What verse(s) in the Old Testament did this fulfill?

_____

7. What scriptures teach that Jesus was offered as a sacrifice to God according to a predetermined plan?

_____

_____

8. Was the exact procedure to the precise detail of Jesus' crucifixion foreknown? What are some Old Testament verses which tell us of particular events?

_____

_____

_____

_____

Chapter 9

Restoration by the Blood

Without contradiction Job is the oldest book in the Bible, and what took place occurred long before the Law was given. In this ancient book we see the Blood message beautifully taught, although by a natural study apart from the Holy Spirit it would be impossible to grasp this message. There are many interpretations, and widely differing views concerning the book of Job. It is not our purpose to bring these forth or comment on the philosophical implications. Our study is concentrated on salvation and restoration by the Blood, and from the first and last chapter of Job, we will draw our discussion.

The Hedge

Job was a man who believed in and offered blood sacrifices. Satan would have smitten Job years before he did but was prevented by what the devil himself called a 'hedge'. Standing before God to give an account of his walks upon earth, the adversary

> 'answered the LORD, and said, "Does Job fear God for nothing? Have You not made a **hedge** around

> *him, around his household, and around all that he*
> *has on every side? You have blessed the work of his*
> *hands, and his possessions have increased in the*
> *land."'* (Job 1:9–10)

The hedge of divine protection was in response to Job's burnt offerings which he offered continually (Job 1:5) and guarded five areas: Job's person, Job's house and family, Job's possessions, Job's endeavors, and Job's influence.

Our blood protection today is a hedge that guards us on every side. Our **hedge protection** insures us of continued blessing from God. It is my opinion that today in the New Covenant, our protection is guaranteed in the blood of Christ and is not withdrawn from us at any time if we meet the conditions.

In this day of salvation only a believer can break his hedge. *'. . . whoso breaketh an hedge, a serpent shall bite him'* (Ecclesiastes 10:8). The serpent cannot bite one who does not break his hedge. Today the adversary tempts us to disobedience that we might break our hedge. The believer who does not rule well over his own life is like a city broken down and without walls. He has no protection from satanic invasion (see Proverbs 25:28).

Job: The Priest of His Home

The Scriptures teach that a husband/father has the responsibility to provide for his family. This is true in the spiritual as well as the natural. The father sprinkled blood over his home in the behalf of his firstborn and family (see Exodus 12). The Philippian jailer was a husband and a father. Paul and Silas addressed this head of a home saying, *'Believe on the Lord Jesus*

*Christ, and thou shalt be saved, **and thy house.'** (Acts 16:31). Job was acting on this principle long ago when he offered burnt sacrifices for his children:

> *'Now his sons would go and feast in their houses, each on his appointed day, and would send and invite their three sisters to eat and drink with them. So it was, when the days of feasting had run their course, that Job would send and sanctify them, and he would rise early in the morning and offer burnt offerings according to the number of them all. For Job said, "It may be that my sons have sinned and cursed God in their hearts." Thus Job did regularly.'*
> (Job 1:4–5)

We have previously seen how Cain and Abel did not offer sacrifice until they left home. In the same manner, Job provided a blood covering for his sons and daughters all the while during his prosperity. There came a day when the hedge was removed. First, his business and then his children were destroyed.

Twice As Much

We now leave Job chapter one and go to the end of the book. In chapter 42, the Lord reproves Job's three friends for their wrong remarks. He instructs them,

> *'Therefore take unto you now seven bullocks and seven rams, and go to my servant Job, and offer for yourselves a burnt offering; and my servant Job shall pray for you: for him will I accept.'* (Job 42:8)

As the three friends offered the sacrifice,[1] and the Lord accepted Job through the blood, the hedge was restored. The protection Job had known prior to the trial was once again in operation, but only after the sacrifices were offered.

> *'And the* LORD *turned the captivity of Job, when he prayed for his friends:* [2] *also the Lord gave Job **twice as much** as he had before.'* (Job 42:10)

In Job 1:3, Job had 7,000 sheep, 3,000 camels, 500 yoke of oxen, and 500 she asses. In Job 42:12 where the Lord blessed the latter end of Job more than his beginning, he had twice the number of animals as he had before.

> *'So the* LORD *blessed the latter end of Job more than his beginning: for he had fourteen thousand sheep, and six thousand camels, and a thousand yoke of oxen, and a thousand she asses.'* (Job 42:12)

Everything Job had lost was restored to him double. We are restored in Christ 'much more' than what we would have had only in Adam.

Salvation by the Blood

Not only had Job lost his cattle. **He also lost his seven sons and three daughters.** *'And there were born unto him seven sons and three daughters'* (Job 1:2). They died in a windstorm near the beginning of Job's calamities (see Job 1:18–19). At the end of the trial God, we are told, restored **twice as much** of everything Job lost. Following the same order Job would have **fourteen sons and six daughters** born to him to replace the seven sons and three daughters lost at the beginning of the book of Job. Look at chapter 42, however, and see how many sons and daughters he had following the turning of his captivity. *'He had also seven sons and three daughters'* (Job 42:13). Here is a beautiful truth. God did not give Job twice the number of sons and daughters **because the first set of sons and daughters were atoned for by the blood**. Job had not lost them because they were saved! Job did actually have fourteen sons and six daughters. The first half were in Paradise[3] and the second half were born to him in the restoration of 'twice as much' of everything that he had had. He did get double the number of cattle for when an animal dies it ceases to exist.

The children who died in chapter 1 did not cease to exist. They were covered by Job's blood sacrifices and were accepted into Paradise. Therefore he got only the same number of sons and daughters (chapter 42) because he had not really lost the first seven sons and three daughters. Meditate on this and you will see a beautiful type of salvation by the Blood. *'... the LORD gave Job twice as much as he had before.'*

Additional Notes

1. No sacrifices were offered from chapters 2 through 41. Perhaps this is the reason Satan destroyed Job's cattle and why the Lord told his friends to provide the sacrifice in chapter 42.
2. Job's friends had misjudged Job and had spoken incorrectly of the Lord. When Job prayed for them, he was acting upon the New Covenant concept of forgiveness.
3. Also known as 'Abraham's Bosom' after the patriarch died.

Questions on Chapter 9

1. Is blood sacrifice taught in Job?

    _____

2. What prevented Satan from attacking Job years
    before he was finally permitted to?

    _____

3. What five areas of Job's concerns were under
    divine protection?

    _____

    _____

4. Can Satan attack us if we are willfully
    disobedient to God? Why?

    _____

    _____

5. What verse in Acts did Job exemplify when he
    offered burnt offerings for his children?

    _____

6. What did Job do for his friends after they offered
    animal sacrifices to the Lord in chapter 42 that
    would demonstrate forgiveness for the wrong
    things they had said?

    _____

    _____

7. How much did God restore to Job? (Three
    words.)

    _____

8.   Did Job, in actual fact, have twice the number of
     sons and daughters from man's natural point of
     view? _____

     How then did God give him twice as much as he
     had before?

     _____

     _____

     _____

     _____

Chapter 10

The Blood of the New Covenant

Some Basics About Covenant

The Old Testament Hebrew word *berith* means 'to cut; to cut asunder' (*Wilson's Old Testament Word Studies*). It is frequently the object of *karath*, 'to divide or cut in two' (*Vine's Expository Dictionary*).

The New Testament Greek word is *daitheke* and refers to a testament [1] or will. The death of the 'testator' (the writer of the testament) was required before the conditions and the effects of his will could be known and realized.

A basic covenant involved a pact, or promise, between two parties in which each pledged to the other all his possessions, strength, etc., and which was sealed with the shedding of blood. The best book I have seen, which exhaustively explores ancient blood covenants of many primitive peoples around the world, is the excellent study by H. Clay Trumbull, *The Blood Covenant*, (republished in 1975 by Impact Books, 137 W. Jefferson, Kirkwood, MO 63122). He shows how the pure blood covenant concept was perverted in paganism, but is fully realized in the better covenant Jesus Christ effected at the cross.

I will only point out that there are many valid

examples of blood covenanting between men in the Old Testament. In fact, the first time the word *berith* appears in reference to man-to-man covenants concerns Mamre, Aner, and Eschol who were 'confederate' (in covenant) with Abram (see Genesis 14:13). Next appears Abraham's covenant with King Abimelech (see Genesis 21:22–34), followed by the continuation of the covenant between their sons, younger Abimelech and Isaac (see Genesis 26:26–33). Jacob and Laban covenanted with each other (see Genesis 31:43–54) which settled their previous animosity. Jonathan and David made a covenant, out of their love for one another, which David honored years after Jonathan's tragic death, in that he seated crippled Mephibosheth, Jonathan's remaining son, at the royal table (see 1 Samuel 18:1–4, 20:4–17; 2 Samuel 9). (There is a common error about this particular covenant which is reproved in the appendix.)

Although peoples of other cultures cut their wrists and even drank their blood and/or animal's blood (as Trumbull points out), this practice was never observed among Hebrews who made individual covenants. They halved prized animals, and passed between the parts, sealing their covenants with one another (one Hebrew word for 'covenant' [*karath*] has to do with 'dividing into parts' and apparently comes from the ceremony described in Genesis 15:9–17 in which God appeared as *'a smoking furnace, and a burning lamp that passed between those pieces'*).

This practice is alluded to in Jeremiah 34:18 concerning covenanters who transgressed their covenant with God:

> *'And I will give* [to destruction] *the men that have transgressed My covenant, which have not performed*

the words of the covenant which they made [literally, "cut"] *before Me when they **cut the calf in twain, and passed between the parts thereof**.'*

The human covenants were permanent, binding, and even perpetual (from generation to generation). They were **fair** as each pledged the same to the other. There are no fewer than eight covenants between God and men in the Bible. It cannot be said, in all honesty, that a parity of fairness could possibly exist in a covenant between the divine and the human.

Concerning this fact, W.E. Vine remarked:

'The word "covenant" in its sense of an agreement on the part of two contracting parties cannot apply to a covenant between God and man. His covenant is essentially a matter of grace on His part (compare Galatians 3). Accordingly, in Psalm 89:28 God's covenant is explained by the accompanying statement of His mercy. Similarly with God's covenant not to destroy the earth again by water (Genesis 9:15). So with regard to His covenant with David and with the Levites, the priests, His ministers (Jeremiah 33:20–22).'

(Vine's Expository Dictionary, p. 53)

God established covenants between Himself and:
1. Noah (Genesis 6:18–21, 8:20–22, 9:9–17; Isaiah 54:9, 10)
2. Abraham (Genesis 15:7–17, 17:1–14; Romans 4; Galatians 3) (reaffirmed to Isaac and Jacob)
3. Israel (Exodus 24:4–8; Hebrews 9:18–20) (This was called the Law Covenant/Old Covenant – Moses was the mediator.)
4. David (Psalm 89:20–37)

5. Hezekiah (2 Chronicles 29:3–36)
6. Jehoida (2 Kings 11:17–20)
7. Josiah (2 Chronicles 34:29–33)
8. The Church (Luke 22:20–21; Hebrews 8, 9, 10 *et al.* (This is called the Grace Covenant/ New Covenant/Better Covenant – Jesus is the mediator.)

Where Is the New Covenant?

The scene is the Last Supper during which Jesus eats the Passover with His disciples before He suffers. He has taken the bread and given it to them saying, *'This is My body which is given for you: this do in remembrance of Me.'* As He prepares to give them the cup He says, *'This cup is the New Testament in My blood, which is shed for you'* (Luke 22:20). Mark the words: *'the New Testament in My blood.'* The New Covenant is ratifed, enacted, resident, and sealed in the blood of Jesus Christ. *'This is the blood of the New Testament.'* (Mark 14:24). Without the blood there is no possible way He could have established a New Covenant between God and man. The New Testament (covenant, agreement, pact, promise, economy) is founded and based on the blood of Jesus.

The Blood Makes the Covenant

The Old Covenant between Yahweh and Israel was dedicated with blood. The transaction is recorded in Exodus 24. An insight into what really happened at that time is revealed in Hebrews 9:18–20:

> *'Therefore not even the first covenant was dedicated without blood. For when Moses had spoken every*

precept to all the people according to the law, he took the blood of calves and goats, with water, scarlet wool, and hyssop, and sprinkled both the book itself and all the people, saying, "This is the blood of the covenant which God has commanded you."'

First Moses sprinkled the book that contained the Law of God. Sprinkling the blood upon the written record bound God to His Word. Then Moses sprinkled all the people with blood. This bound Israel to the covenant by the blood. An alternate rendering of verse 20 is: **'This is the blood that makes the covenant by which God is joined to you.' God was joined to Israel by the blood that made the covenant.**

The written record of the New Covenant is likewise sprinkled with blood. When a translator takes the Blood out of the pages of the New Testament he is removing the seal of God from his translation. There are some new translations on the market today not worthy of our consideration. When the blood is taken out of the Scriptures the life of God is removed. The Greek word *haima* should be translated 'blood' and not 'death' or 'sacrifice'.

John writes,

'And there are three that bear witness in earth, the (Holy) Spirit, and the water (of the Word), and the blood (of Christ): and these three agree in one.'

(1 John 5:8)

The Spirit, the Word, and the Blood give testimony concerning God and His program to men on earth. **These three agree in one**; they cannot be divorced from the other. Each has no function apart from the other two and must be seen as one unity. When one is removed the other two are removed as well. The churches that have removed the Blood from their songs have taken the Spirit out of their worship. The Holy Spirit agrees with the blood of Christ. Theologians who have banished the Blood from their teaching are no longer teaching God's Word. The Word and the Blood agree.

The legal grounds for all of God's provisions rests upon the basis of the blood of Christ. The Word provides the information on what these provisions are and instruction on how to enter into them. The Holy Spirit, as the divine administrator over all of God's blessings, ministers these provisions into our lives. One is not sufficient by itself. These three work together to give testimony to men.

The Blood of Access

And then in similar comparision we, as Israel was, are likewise sprinkled with the Blood. Just as the blood binds God to His people through His Word, the blood binds the people to God through His Word. The Spirit seals this operation. The Spirit bears witness to our spirit affirming that we are in the covenant. We are ushered before God's presence by the Holy Spirit according to the Word when sprinkled with Christ's blood.

Peter describes this sprinkling.

> '*Elect according to the foreknowledge of God the Father, through sanctification of the Spirit, unto obedience and* **sprinkling of the blood of Jesus Christ**.'
> (1 Peter 1:2)

151

Thus sprinkled, our basis of approach to God is guaranteed.

> *'Having therefore, brethren, boldness to enter into the holiest* (Holy of Holies) **by the blood of Jesus**, *by a new and living way, which He hath consecrated for us, through the veil, that is to say, His flesh . . . '*
> (Hebrews 10:19–20)

The veil that separated the Holy of Holies from the Holy Place (in the earthly temple) was torn from top to bottom after Jesus bore our sins upon Calvary.

Immediately following the death of Jesus this 60-foot tall veil in the Herodian temple [2] was rent in twain from top to bottom showing the rending had to be from above. If men had torn the veil it would have been torn from the bottom upwards. This was an act of God showing that the partition that separated man from a free access of approach to the Father was now gone.

> *'And, behold, the veil of the temple was rent in twain from the top to the bottom.'* (Matthew 27:51)

A man can now approach God without human intermediary (priests, etc.) for Jesus has gone ahead as the forerunner and prepared the way. Jesus is now the High Priest and every believer is a priest. **Unrestricted access to God and unhindered fellowship with Him is available to all who come by the blood of Jesus.** This new and living way is the substance of what the old ceremonial way foreshadowed. In the Old Covenant only one man could go once a year whereas in the New Covenant all may come daily.

> *'Let us therefore come boldly unto the throne of grace, that we may obtain mercy, and find grace to help in time of need.'* (Hebrews 4:16)

We do not approach in fear of death as did the high priest under the Law. We come **boldly** to obtain help from the Throne.

A Better Covenant

If the first covenant had been faultless there would have been no need for a second (see Hebrews 8:7).

> *'But now hath He obtained a much more excellent ministry, by how much also He is the mediator of a better covenant which was established upon better promises.'* (Hebrews 8:6)

As a high priest Jesus has a much more excellent ministry to God on our behalf for He does not offer the blood of bulls and goats which cannot take away sin (see Hebrews 10:4), but pleads our case to the Father by the merit of His own sacrifice. Our Priest is our Sacrifice. He intercedes for us on the basis of His eternal blood and is thus able to save to the uttermost (see Hebrews 7:25).

The New Covenant is better than the old for the Blood that enacted it is better blood. The blood of bulls and goats could only sanctify ceremonially. The blood of Christ purges even the **conscience** of the believer (see Hebrews 9:13–14). Through the Blood of the New Covenant we have full access to God at all times. By His blood Jesus entered into the Holiest of

All in heaven and there intercedes in the place of full favor at the Father's right hand.

> *'For Christ is not entered into the holy places made with hands* (earthly tabernacle/temple built by men), ***which are figures of the true; but into heaven itself***, *now to appear in the presence of God for us: Nor yet that He should offer Himself often, as the high priest entereth into the holy place every year with the blood of others . . . '* (Hebrews 9:24–25)

Jesus entered **heaven itself** there to appear before God **for us** not with the blood of others, but with His own blood. The earthly patterns (wilderness tabernacle) were of necessity purified with the blood of animals. But the heavenly things (mercy-seat before the throne; corresponding to the mercy-seat between the cherubim) were sanctified with better Blood. Hebrews 9:22–23 tells us:

> *'And almost all things are by the law purged with blood; and without shedding of blood is no remission. It was therefore necessary that the patterns of things in the heavens should be purified with these; but the heavenly things themselves with better sacrifices than these.'*

In heaven our Great High Priest fulfilled the sprinkling of Blood on the mercy-seat in the same manner that the earthly high priest annually sprinkled the blood of one sin offering on behalf of Israel.

> *'Then shall he . . . bring His blood within the veil . . . and sprinkle it upon the mercy seat, and before the*

> *mercy seat: And he shall make an atonement . . . for all the congregation of Israel.'* (Leviticus 16:15–17)

When the blood was sprinkled seven times (Leviticus 16:14) on the mercy-seat and the ceremony completed, the Day of Atonement resulted in a blood covering for a full year for the Israelites. **The blood of bulls and goats accomplished an annual covering or atonement,** *while the blood of Christ has accomplished eternal redemption for the Church.*

> *'But Christ being come an high priest of good things to come, by a greater and more perfect tabernacle, not made with hands, that is to say, not of this building; neither by the blood of goats and calves, but by His own blood He entered in once into the holy place, having obtained eternal redemption for us.'*
> (Hebrews 9:11–12)

> *'But ye are come unto . . .* **the blood of sprinkling** *that speaketh better things than that of Abel.'*
> (Hebrews 12:22, 24)

Jesus does not come before the Father once a year. He lives continually at the Father's right hand making intercession for the saints. We are saved from 'the guttermost to the uttermost' when we come unto God by Him. Jesus lives, 'after the power of an endless life' (Hebrews 7:16). 'Endless' means 'indestructible, inexhaustible, and unending'.

Due to the fact that Jesus plainly said the new covenant is in His blood, every provision in this pact is based upon His blood. How true it is that every provision of God that we enjoy in this new and living way was automatically ratified by the blood of Christ. We will now consider how the four main provisions are directly related to the Blood.

Forgiveness of sin is based directly on the blood of Jesus.

> *'In Whom we have redemption through His blood, the forgiveness of sins, according to the riches of his grace.'* (Ephesians 1:7)

> *'In Whom we have redemption through His blood, even the forgiveness of sins.'* (Colossians 1:14)

> *'and without shedding of blood is no remission* (forgiveness).' (Hebrews 9:22)

Holiness of heart and life is based directly on the Blood.

> *'But if we walk in the light, as He is in the light, we have fellowship one with another, and the blood of Jesus Christ His Son cleanseth us from all sin.'* (1 John 1:7)

> *'Wherefore Jesus also, that He might sanctify the people with His own blood, suffered without the gate.'* (Hebrews 13:12)

Healing for the body was obtained by the blood that flowed from His back.

> *'Surely He hath borne our sicknesses, and carried our pains.'* (Isaiah 53:4)

> *'. . . and with His stripes we are healed.'* (Isaiah 53:5)

Each of these statements has the double witness of a New Testament author. Matthew confirmed the message of Isaiah 53:4:

> *'That it might be fulfilled which was spoken by Esaias* (Isaiah) *the prophet, saying, Himself took our infirmities, and bare our sicknesses.'*
>
> (Matthew 8:17)

Peter confirmed the message of Isaiah 53:5:

> *'... by Whose stripes ye were healed.'* (1 Peter 2:24)

Peter looks over his shoulder some 38 years or so and says, *'were healed.'* Healing is an accomplished fact. To easily observe that we are healed by the blood of Christ one need only recognize the color of the healing stripes. (As the red blood surfaced on the skin the stripes became visible.)

The baptism with the Holy Spirit is pictured in the supernatural sign of the flowing water out of the crucified Christ's side. It was more than the clear fluid that collects in the chest cavity (which is not more than a few tablespoons). This was an actual stream of water that fulfilled the type of the water from the rock in the Old Testament and symbolized the living water Jesus gives to quench our thirst.

> *'But one of the soldiers with a spear pierced His side and forthwith came there out blood and water.'*
>
> (John 19:34)

(We develop this thought more fully in the chapter entitled, 'Water From the Rock'.)

The Name of Jesus

It is through the name of Jesus that the believer exercises his authority over demons and sickness (see Mark 16:14–18). It is in Jesus' name that we present our needs to the Father (see John 14:13–14, 16:23–24). If Jesus had not accomplished the will of God and had not established this new covenant in His blood, His name would have no power. There are two scriptures which infer that the Name has its authority on the basis of the Blood.

> *'For where a testament is, there must also of necessity be the death of the testator.'*   (Hebrews 9:16)

Jesus is the testator (covenant-maker) of the New Testament. It was necessary that He die, and that He die shedding His blood. Had He not done this the New Covenant would not have come into force. The name of the testator would not be effectual. The name of Jesus is effectual because of the death and resurrection of the Testator. The name of Jesus and its authority is a part of the overall covenant.

The second scripture which reveals the authority of the name based on the Blood is Luke 10:17–20:

> *'Then the seventy returned with joy, saying, "LORD, even the demons are subject to us in Your name." And He said to them, "I saw Satan fall like lightning from heaven. Behold, I give you the authority to trample on serpents and scorpions, and over all the power of the enemy, and nothing shall by any means hurt you. Nevertheless do not rejoice in this, that the spirits are subject to you, but rather rejoice because your names are written in heaven."'*

The seventy were not to rejoice that the demons were subject unto them but that their names were written in heaven. That is precisely the reason why the demons were subject unto them! The seven sons of Sceva attempted to use the name of Jesus against evil spirits but were most unsuccessful. These Jewish exorcists were not believers in our Lord Jesus. Their names were not written in heaven and the demons did not come out (see Acts 19:13–17). The name of Jesus is ineffectual if the user is not washed from his sins in the Blood knowing his/her name is written in heaven. (The obvious exception is when a sinner prays in Jesus' name for salvation, see Romans 10:13.)

Covenant Comparison

The writer of Hebrews tells us,

> '*He is the mediator of a better covenant, which was established upon better promises.*'   (Hebrews 8:6)

For a fuller understanding of the better qualities resident in the New Covenant as compared to the Old, we have provided a columnar comparison between the mechanics and operations of the two covenants. We have shown twelve main points of difference between the old and new covenants and given the scripture references to establish these points.

Old Covenant	New Covenant
1. Was ratified by the blood of bulls and goats (Exodus 24:8; Hebrews 9:19–20).	1. Was ratified by the better blood of Jesus Christ (Luke 22:20).

2. Provided only an annual covering on the Day of Atonement (Leviticus 16:12–19).

2. Obtained an eternal redemption for us (Hebrews 9:12).

3. High priest entered the Holiest once a year and remained there only a short time (Leviticus 16:30, 34; Hebrews 9:7, 25).

3. Christ entered the Holiest in heaven and ministers there as High Priest continually (Hebrews 10:12, 8:2, 7:24–25, 6:20).

4. High priest entered the Holiest without boldness in fear of death (Leviticus 16:2).

4. Jesus destroyed the devil who had the power of death and delivered those who through fear of death were all their life-time subject to bondage (Hebrews 2:14–15).

5. No other Israelite was permitted to enter the Holiest ever – not even other priests (Hebrews 9:6–7).

5. All brethren should have boldness to enter the Holiest by the blood of Jesus, by a new and living way which He has consecrated for us through His flesh (Hebrews 10:19–23).

6. Could not take away sins and cleansed only the outward (Hebrews 1:4, 9:13).

6. Cleanses from all sin and purges the conscience of the worshiper (Hebrews 9:14; 1 John 1:7, 9)

7. The Veil separated from God's presence (Hebrews 9:3–5).

7. The Veil was supernaturally torn in half exposing the Holiest (Matthew 27:51; Hebrews 6:19–20, 9:8).

8. God has made the first covenant old and ready to vanish away. He promised those living under this covenant that He would make a new one (Hebrews 8:8–13).

8. God has accepted Christ's sacrifice and made this the Everlasting Covenant in which His promise to Abraham is fulfilled (Hebrews 13:20; Galatians 3:29).

160

9. The Law is good in that it provides shadows of the work of Christ but no longer provides a means of access to God (Hebrews 10:1).

9. Christ is the end of the Law for righteousness to everyone that believes (Romans 10:4).

10. In the end never made anyone perfect (Galatians 3:11; Hebrews 10:1–2).

10. The Great Shepherd through the blood of the Everlasting Covenant makes the Christian perfect in every good work to do His will (Hebrews 13:21).

11. The high priests died and were replaced (Hebrews 7:23–25).

11. Jesus lives after the power of an endless, indestructible, resurrection life (Hebrews 7:16).

12. At death a righteous Israelite departed to Abraham's Bosom known as Paradise in Sheol/Hades (Luke 16:22).

12. At death the believer departs to be in the presence of the Lord (with Christ) which is far better (2 Corinthians 5:8; Philippians 1:21–23).

In the light of the above scriptural comparisons, is it any wonder that the writer of Hebrews calls the New Covenant a 'better' one?

Additional Notes

1. Although the stricter meaning of 'testament' does not convey the fuller meaning of 'covenant' inasmuch as a testament does not necessitate a mutual commitment between two parties.
2. Alfred Eidersheim, in his fascinating work: *The Life and Times of Jesus the Messiah* (MacDonald Publishing Co., McLean, VA), said, 'The Veils before the Most Holy Place were 40 cubits (60 feet) long, and 20 (30 feet) wide, of the thickness of the palm of

the hand, and wrought in 72 squares, which were joined together; and these Veils were so heavy, that, in the exaggerated language of the time, it needed 300 priests to manipulate each. If the Veil was at all such as is described in the Talmud, it could not have been rent in twain by a mere earthquake or the fall of the lintel, although its composition in squares fastened together might explain, how the rent might be as described in the Gospel ... the rent of the Temple-Veil was − with reverence be it said − really made by the Hand of God' (Book V, p. 611).

Questions on Chapter 10

1. What does the Hebrew word *berith* mean?

   _____

2. What does the Greek word *diatheke* mean?

   _____

3. Did a basic covenant involve a pact, or promise,
   between two parties? _____ Name at least two
   covenants between men in the Old Testament:

   _____

   _____

4. Did Hebrews cut their wrists and mingle their
   blood together, and/or even drink a little of it?
   _____ What did they cut to signify their
   covenant?

   _____

   _____

5. God established no fewer than _____ covenants
   between Himself and men.

6. Name at least four individuals with whom God
   established a covenant:

   _____

   _____

   _____

   _____

7. Where is the New Covenant?

   _____

8. (Fill in the blanks): 'First Moses sprinkled the
    _____ that contained the Law of God . . .
    Then, Moses sprinkled all the _____ with
    blood.'

9. 1 John 5:8 says there are how many that bear
    witness in earth?

    _____

10. How should the Greek word *haima* be translated?

    _____

11. What scripture in the New Testament actually
    says we are *sprinkled* with the blood of Christ?

    _____

12. The high priest was permitted to enter the Most
    Holy Place only one time a year. How often may
    we enter the Holiest of All according to Hebrews
    4:16, 10:19? _____ Upon what basis may
    we enter?

    _____

13. The Veil in the Herodian Temple was _____
    feet tall.

14. Did Jesus enter in the earthly Holy of Holies?
    _____ If not, where did He go?

    _____

15. Name at least three provisions of the New
    Covenant which are directly based upon Jesus'
    blood:

    _____

    _____

16. Why cannot an unbeliever use the Name of Jesus to rebuke the devil?

   _____

   _____

17. The Old Covenant was ratified by the blood of animal sacrifices. *True or False?*

18. The Great High Priest of our confession, Jesus Christ, must continually offer sin sacrifices in heaven because His one sacrifice on the cross was not enough. *True or False?*

19. No other person besides the high priest was permitted to enter the Holy of Holies. *True or False?*

20. At death a righteous Israelite was 'absent from the body and present with the Lord' due to the fact that animal blood could take away sin. *True or False?*

21. The blood of Jesus cleanses away sin and purges the inner man's conscience. *True or False?*

22. God promised He would make a New Covenant during the period that the Old Covenant was still in effect. *True or False?*

Chapter 11

Descriptions of the Blood

The Blood Characteristics Are Ours

Jesus was cursed on the tree in our place and bore our sin in His own body (see Galatians 3:13; 1 Peter 2:24). He did not bear our sin in His blood. It was just as holy on the cross as it ever was. As He offered the sin sacrifice to God, He was covered with pure, innocent, justifying, redeeming, sanctifying Blood so that He was able to dismiss His spirit to the Father at death. He was drenched in His blood just as the living bird was dipped in the blood of the dead bird (Leviticus 14:6). For this reason His body was raised the third day and saw no corruption whatever.

The blood of Jesus is often preceded by a descriptive adjective in the Scriptures or a verse in which an adjective could be used to describe the nature and work of His blood. The adjectives given below do not always appear in that form in the verse, but for our study they may be employed. We have limited our comments on these verses and would recommend that the student confess the blood with the adjective preceding it to realize what kind of blood Jesus shed for us. Example: 'the justifying blood'.

Justifying

'Much more then, being now **justified by His blood**, we shall be saved from wrath through Him.'

(Romans 5:9)

Redeeming

'And they sung a new song, saying, Thou art worthy to take the book, and to open the seals thereof: for Thou wast slain, and hast **redeemed us to God by Thy blood** out of every kindred, and tongue, and people, and nation.' (Revelation 5:9)

'In Whom we have **redemption through His blood** . . .' (Ephesians 1:7; Colossians 1:14)

Remitting

'And almost all things are by the law purged with blood; and **without shedding of blood is no remission.**' (Hebrews 9:22)

Forgiving

'In whom we have redemption through His blood, **the forgiveness of sins**, according to the riches of His grace . . .' (Ephesians 1:7)

'In Whom we have redemption through His blood, even **the forgiveness of sins** . . .' (Colossians 1:14)

Washing and freeing

'And from Jesus Christ, who is the faithful witness, and the first begotten of the dead, and the prince of the kings of the earth. Unto Him that loved us and **washed us from our sins in His own blood.**'

(Revelation 1:5)

Washed is also translated *'freed'*. When a garment is soiled, the dirt is freed from it as it is washed.

Purging

> *'How much more shall the blood of Christ, who through the eternal Spirit offered Himself without spot to God, **purge your conscience** from dead works to serve the living God?'* (Hebrews 9:14)

Cleansing

> *'But if we walk in the light, as He is in the light, we have fellowship one with another, and the blood of Jesus Christ His Son **cleanseth us from all sin**.'*
> (1 John 1:7)

Sanctifying

> *'Wherefore Jesus also, that He might **sanctify the people with His own blood**, suffered without the gate.'* (Hebrews 13:12)

Reconciling

> *'But now in Christ Jesus ye who sometimes were far off are **made nigh by the blood of Christ**.'*
> (Ephesians 2:13)

Blotting

> *'**Blotting out the handwriting of ordinances that was against us**, which was contrary to us, and took it out of the way, nailing it to His cross . . .'*
> (Colossians 2:14)

Triumphing

> 'And having spoiled principalities and powers, He made a shew of them openly, **triumphing over them in it**.'
> (Colossians 2:15)

'Spoiled' can be translated 'divested Himself of' or 'disarmed'. This means Christ divested Satan of his authority. He completely disarmed all of his powers. Satan is a snake with a crushed head. Jesus fulfilled the first prophecy concerning the Messiah that was spoken directly to the serpent.

> 'And I will put enmity between thee and the woman, and between thy seed and her seed; it shall bruise thy head, and thou shalt bruise His heel.'
> (Genesis 3:15)

Satan bruised Christ's heel with the sting of death at the cross whereby Jesus **crushed** the snake's head (literal meaning of 'bruise'). Jesus disarmed the enemy of all his power so that He could say prior to the Ascension, *'All power is given unto Me in heaven and in earth'* (Matthew 28:18).

> 'For this purpose the Son of God was manifested, that He may destroy the works of the devil.'
> (1 John 3:8)

Through His death Jesus rendered helpless him that had the power of death, that is, the devil (see Hebrews 2:14–15). The only power the snake with a crushed head has today is the power of deception (see John 8:44). When a believer refuses to accept his lies, the enemy has no hold on him.

Overcoming

> *'And they **overcame him by the blood of the Lamb**, and by the word of their testimony; and they loved not their lives unto the death.'*   (Revelation 12:11)

Whenever a believer vocally agrees with God's attitude toward the blood of Jesus, he or she at once overcomes the accuser's attacks upon the mind.

Agreeing

> *'And there are three that bear witness in earth, the Spirit, and the water, and the blood: and **these three agree in one.'***   (1 John 5:8)

Communing

> *'The cup of blessing which we bless, is it not **the communion of the blood** of Christ? The bread which we break, is it not the communion of the body of Christ?'*   (1 Corinthians 10:16)

The body of Christ must base its fellowship among the members upon the basis of the blood of Christ. The Blood provides the basis of fellowship with other believers (see 1 John 1:7). The Church is full of 'seditions' – a work of the flesh for ignoring the communion of the Blood (see Galatians 5:20). The word 'communion' is *koinonia* and means 'association, joint-participation, sharing and fellowship' (abridged from *Thayer's*).

Purchasing

> *'...feed the church of God, which He hath **purchased with His own blood.'***   (Acts 20:28)

Sprinkling

> *'And to Jesus the mediator of the new covenant, and to **the blood of sprinkling**, that speaketh better things than that of Abel.'*   (Hebrews 12:24)

> *'Elect according to the foreknowledge of God the Father, through sanctification of the Spirit, unto obedience and **sprinkling of the blood** of Jesus Christ...'*   (1 Peter 1:2)

Speaking

> *'... that **speaketh better things** than that of Abel.'*
> (Hebrews 12:24)

If His blood is yet speaking, it is still living.

Whitening

> *'These ... have washed their robes and made them **white** in the blood of the Lamb. Therefore are they before the throne of God...'*   (Revelation 7:14–15)

Peacemaking

> *'And, having made **peace** through the blood of His cross, by Him to reconcile all things unto Himself...'*   (Colossians 1:20)

Incorruptible

> *'Forasmuch as ye know that ye were not redeemed with **corruptible** things, as silver and gold, from your vain conversation received by tradition from your fathers.'*   (1 Peter 1:18)

Since we are not redeemed with corruptible things and are redeemed by the Blood, it is incorruptible blood.

Precious

'But with **the precious blood** of Christ, as of a lamb without blemish and without spot . . . ' (1 Peter 1:19)

Holy

'Of how much sorer punishment, suppose ye, shall he be thought worthy, who hath trodden under foot the Son of God, and **hath counted the blood** of the covenant, wherewith he was sanctified, **an unholy thing**, and hath done despite unto the Spirit of grace?'
(Hebrews 10:29)

It is wrong to count the Blood an unholy thing, because it is holy blood.

Atoning

'For the life of the flesh is in the blood: and I have given it to you upon the altar to make an atonement for your souls; for it is **the blood** that **maketh an atonement** for the soul.' (Leviticus 17:11)

Innocent

'Saying, I have sinned in that I have betrayed **the innocent blood**.' (Matthew 27:4)

Notice the article 'the' before 'innocent blood' – His was the only **totally** innocent blood in all respects!

Accessing

'Having therefore, brethren, boldness to enter into **the holiest by the blood of Jesus**.' (Hebrews 10:19)

Perfect

> *'When Jesus therefore had received the vinegar, He said, **It is finished**; and He bowed His head, and gave up the ghost* (spirit).'*   (John 19:30)

'Finished' means perfect and complete. 'It' refers to His blood sacrifice. His eyes saw the Blood that drenched all about Him. His body, the cross, and the ground were covered with the Blood.

Sheltering

> *'For the LORD will pass through to smite the Egyptians; and **when He seeth the blood** upon the lintel, and on the two side posts, **the LORD will pass** (as a guard) **over the door, and will not suffer** (permit) **the destroyer to come in** unto your houses to smite you.'*
>   (Exodus 12:23)

Shed

> *'Likewise also the cup after supper, saying, This cup is the new testament in **My blood**, which **is shed** for you.'*   (Luke 22:20)

Thank God, it wasn't *spilled* by accident, but *shed* on purpose.

Saving

> *'As for thee also, by the blood of thy covenant I have sent forth thy prisoners out of the pit wherein is no water.'*   (Zechariah 9:11)

Zechariah speaks to those living in the New Covenant time period. We were prisoners of the devil and were headed for the pit which has no water. In God's eyes we were already condemned to the pit because we were members of the kingdom of darkness. When we were translated into the kingdom of His dear Son we were positionally removed from the judgment unto the second death which is the lake of fire. This has occurred by the blood of our better covenant which Zechariah foresaw.

The Scriptures teach that *a person is whatever the Blood is* when he is covered with it. Take each of these adjectives and confess you are what they are. Example: 'I am redeemed because the redeeming blood covers me. I am saved because the saving blood covers me. I am protected because the sheltering blood covers me.' We were guilty, but when 'the innocent blood' covered us, we were made innocent.

What Happens to Sin?

Many defeated Christians have never learned how to overcome the attacks of the accuser because they are ignorant as to what happens to sin after they have confessed and forsaken it. They have been taught how they are cleansed, but not taught what God does to our transgressions.

By studying what God does to confessed sin and seeing the dramatic change of sin when it is removed, the enemy will be totally unable to torment a believer with his regrettable past. It is God's desire that none of His children live under condemnation (see Romans 8:1).

Confessed sin is *blotted out* so that it is no longer visible in the sight of God.

> *'I, even I, am He that blotteth out thy transgressions for Mine own sake, and will not remember thy sins.'*
> (Isaiah 43:25)

Jesus accomplished this on the tree,

> *'Blotting out the handwriting of ordinances that was against us, which was contrary to us, and took it out of the way, nailing it to His cross.'*
>
> (Colossians 2:14)

This blotting out of sins is pictured as a fog separating between the believer and his past:

> *'I have blotted out, as a thick cloud, thy transgressions, and, as a cloud, thy sins: return unto Me; for I have redeemed thee.'* (Isaiah 44:22)

A thick cloud on ground level is known as a fòg. 'The fog was so thick it blanketed the city.' **This thick cloud has blanketed our forgiven past.** Yet how often the Christian desperately tries to gaze into his past.

It is important to remember that God will not remember the sins He has forgiven. When God forgives He also forgets.

> *'And their sins and iniquities will I remember no more.'* (Hebrews 10:17)

God has **forgotten** our sins promising, *'I will not remember your sins.'* The Word does not say that God **cannot** recall our sins, but rather, He said He **will not** recall them. He has drawn a curtain behind which all our sins are forgotten never to be remembered against us again.

Just because God has forgotten our sins does not mean Satan has. He still remembers our yielding to his temptations and attempts to place regret and guilt upon us by causing us to remember them. Why should we care if the devil remembers anyway? We will answer to God and must please only Him. Our Advocate stills the adversary's voice at this very hour before the throne of God.

Another Bible picture of the doing away of sin is seen in the Psalms. David was instructing his soul to bless the Lord for all His benefits.

> *'Bless the LORD O my soul ... Who forgiveth all thine iniquities ... '* (Psalm 103:1, 3)

The Lord forgives all the iniquities of the soul. Later in the psalm, David mused,

> *'He hath not dealt with us after our sins; nor rewarded us according to our iniquities. For as the heaven is high above the earth, so great is His mercy toward them that fear Him. As far as the east is from the west, so far hath He **removed** our transgressions from us.'* (Psalm 103:10–12)

David did not know what science has learned in fairly recent generations. The Holy Spirit who inspired him knew full well for the Spirit had moved upon the face of the earth (Genesis 1:2). That is, that east and west never meet, but north and south do! If one goes north far enough, he will be heading south after crossing the North Pole. Likewise, if one goes south far enough he will be traveling north after crossing the South Pole. You could travel east forever around this planet and never be heading west and vice-versa. David did not know this.

This verse once more proves the inerrancy of the Scriptures. Had David said, 'As far as the north is from the south, so far hath He removed our transgressions from us,' he would be saying that we would eventually meet our sins again. However, since they are removed as far as the east is from the west, we will never meet with them again. This is actually an immeasurable distance. God *removes* our sins from us.

A third illustration is found in Micah.

> *'Who is a God like unto Thee, that pardoneth iniquity, and passeth by the transgression of the remnant of His heritage? He retaineth not His anger forever, because He delighteth in mercy. He will turn again, He will have compassion upon us; He will subdue our iniquities; and Thou will **cast** all their sins into the depth of the sea.'*
>
> (Micah 7:18–19)

Our sins are **plunged** to the depths of the sea.

Within this century the depth of the sea has been changed time after time. People used to accept three miles as the limit. Later it was changed to five miles deep. During the past few decades, scientists have changed the record twice saying the ocean is seven miles deep, and later over eight miles deep. Only a few hundred feet under the surface and the ocean becomes very dark. Think how impossible it is that the naked eye could view something on the ocean's bottom. It takes specially-built equipment to explore the ocean's depths. Micah shows how far God has removed our sins. In his day it was impossible for anyone to submerge more than the diving depth of the sea. Our sins are plunged far below our remembrance of them, **if we will accept it by faith**.

King Hezekiah was extolling the Lord for His goodness. He had recovered from his terminal sickness and was praising God for the deliverance from death and extension of life. Remembering the sorrow his sickness had brought him, he says,

> *'Behold, for peace I had great bitterness: but Thou hast in love to my soul delivered it from the pit of corruption for Thou hast cast all my sins behind Thy back.'* (Isaiah 38:17)

God has cast all our sins *behind His back*. With the same arm that flung out the planets, our Father has hurled our sins backward, and they are still traveling at the speed of light away from God. Now why is it so important that God has cast our sins behind His back?

> *'God is not a man that He should lie; neither the son of man that He should repent . . . '* (Numbers 23:19)

Because He has cast all our sins behind His back, He will never look upon them again!

Questions on Chapter 11

1. Give at least 25 descriptive adjectives of the Blood
    and the Scripture verses where each is found:

    (1) _____

    (2) _____

    (3) _____

    (4) _____

    (5) _____

    (6) _____

    (7) _____

    (8) _____

    (9) _____

    (10) _____

    (11) _____

    (12) _____

    (13) _____

    (14) _____

    (15) _____

    (16) _____

    (17) _____

    (18) _____

    (19) _____

    (20) _____

    (21) _____

    (22) _____

    (23) _____

    (24) _____

    (25) _____

2. How can we overcome the accuser of the brethren according to Revelation 12:11?

    _____

    _____

    _____

3. Name at least three things God does to confessed sin:

    _____

    _____

    _____

Chapter 12

Water From the Rock

Only a few days into the wilderness and the people of God found no water to drink. Rather than relying on God (who had recently parted the Red Sea) to provide drinking water, they murmured instead against Moses. Here we see the longsuffering and forbearance of God. If He marked our sins, who could stand before Him? (see Psalm 130:3).

After seeking the Lord, Moses took the same rod he had stretched out over the sea and struck the side of a large rock in Horeb. Rivers of water flowed from the inner recesses of this stone, providing water for at least two to three million [1] Israelites.

> *'He opened the rock, and the waters gushed out; they ran in the dry places like a river.'*
>
> (Psalm 105:41)

> *'He split the rocks in the wilderness, and gave them abundant drink like the ocean depths. He brought forth streams also from the rock and caused waters to run down like rivers.'* (Psalm 78:15–16, NASB)

There was an abundant supply of water for the thirsty multitude in the barren wilderness desert. Let's examine carefully the key verse:

> '*Behold, I will stand before thee there upon the rock in Horeb; and thou shalt smite the rock, and **there shall come water out of it**, that the people may drink. And Moses did so in the sight of the elders of Israel.*'
> (Exodus 17:6)

The Lord stood upon the rock picturing that it was He who would perform the supernatural on behalf of His people. The reason God instructed Moses to smite the rock was that Christ, our Rock would be smitten also. '*There shall come water out of it,*' could be rendered 'out of it shall flow water.' Jesus may have had this verse in mind when He stated, '...*as the scripture hath said, Out of his belly shall flow rivers of living water*' (John 7:38). Apparently the only reference in the entire Old Testament was in connection with this particular experience, and the one that followed 38 years later, in the wilderness.

As Moses fulfilled the divine command before the elders of Israel, thousands of gallons of water poured out. There was and is no natural explanation for this tremendous outpouring. It was a supernatural act of God. Those who explain it away with the supposition that Moses struck the weak spot of a cavernous, water-filled rock do not take into account the massive quantities of both man and animal which drank from it.

Paul comments on this wilderness experience in 1 Corinthians. He refers to Israel's passing through the sea, the covering of the cloud, the quail that flew in, and says in reference to the rock in Horeb:

> *'And did all drink the same spiritual drink: for they drank of that spiritual Rock that followed them: and that Rock was Christ.'*   (1 Corinthians 10:4)

That which occurred to the rock in the wilderness also happened to the Rock on the cross. Moses took a rod and smote the side of the rock and water poured out of its side. Notice the parallel with the Rock on the cross,

> *'But one of the soldiers with a spear pierced His side, and forthwith came there out blood **and water**.'*
> (John 19:34)

Likewise Christ was already dead (John 19:30). When He was struck with a spear, and the wilderness rock was, of course, non-living matter. The author believes that the water that poured from Christ's side was as supernaturally created as was the water from Horeb's rock. It was not clear fluid that collects in the chest; **it was a sign from God**. The desert rock provided water for physical thirst. The crucified Rock provided living water for spiritual thirst. Study the columnar illustration following to compare the similarities:

The rock in the desert
(Exodus 17:6)

1. was non-living matter
2. was struck with a rod
3. in the sight of Israel
4. by Moses
5. water flowed out

6. providing drink for murmurers

The Rock on the cross
(John 19:34)

1. was dead
2. was struck with a spear
3. in sight of Jew and Gentile
4. by a soldier
5. blood and water flowed out

6. provided supernatural drink (the Spirit) for praisers

Speak to the Rock

Almost 38 years of wandering in the desert had transpired. Once again Israel found no water. This time history repeated itself as the children of murmurers themselves quarreled with Moses, the weary leader of a stiff-necked people.

On this occasion Moses sadly failed God, preventing his entrance into the promised land:

> 'Then the LORD spoke to Moses, saying, "Take the rod; you and your brother Aaron gather the assembly together. Speak to the rock before their eyes, and it will yield its water; thus you shall bring water for them out of the rock, and give drink to the congregation and their animals." So Moses took the rod from before the LORD as He commanded him. And Moses and Aaron gathered the congregation together before the rock; and he said to them, "Hear now, you rebels! Must we bring water for you out of this rock?" Then Moses lifted his hand and struck the rock twice with his rod; and water came out abundantly, and the congregation and their animals drank. Then the LORD spoke to Moses and Aaron, "Because you did not believe Me, to hallow Me in the eyes of the children of Israel, therefore you shall not bring this congregation into the land which I have given them."'
>
> (Numbers 20:7–12)

Angry toward Israel, Moses disobeyed God's instructions when he:
1. implied that he and Aaron had to provide water
2. addressed Israel instead of speaking to the rock

3. smote the rock twice whereas he was to have taken his rod, the symbol of authority, and to only hold it in his hand!

To **speak** to this rock was all God commanded Moses to do. This would have shown Israel that the rock, having been previously struck, now needed only to be addressed. Speaking to the rock in faith would have caused water to flow as it had some years earlier when smitten. [2]

This rock typifies our Lord Jesus Christ and to smite the rock the second time is the same as crucifying the Son of God afresh. Jesus was smitten once, never to be smitten again. To crucify Christ again would mean His first offering was not enough. However, His first offering was His last for it was perfect.

> *'But this man, after He had offered **one sacrifice** for sins for ever, sat down on the right hand of God.'*
> (Hebrews 10:12)

> *'So Christ was **once offered** to bear the sins of many...'*
> (Hebrews 9:28)

Jesus was crucified once, at which time water poured from His belly. He now sits at the right hand of God and the Holy Spirit proceeds from the throne to the earth as believers speak to the Rock with praise and adoration. To get a drink from Jesus one must not crucify Him the second time but need only worship Him. As we ask in faith we receive.

> *'Open thy mouth wide, and I will fill it.'*
> (Psalm 81:10)

Canaan is a type of the kingdom of God. Moses was not permitted to enter the land of promise because he smote the rock on the second occasion. This is symbolic that one who holds the Son of God to an open shame will be forbidden entrance into the kingdom of God (see Hebrews 6:4–9). Moses' punishment was only figurative of this fact. He was not actually cut off from God; still the punishment was a most tragic one, for Moses had spent most of his life preparing for a land that was closed to him. Moses' disobedience was the most regrettable act of his entire life. We can learn the importance of obeying God from this event.

Drinking of the Spirit

John, the same Gospel writer who also recorded the flowing water from Christ's side was also the sole recorder of the words of Christ depicting this event. Jesus taught that the Holy Spirit would flow from Him to all who thirst, as told in John 7:37–39:

> *'In the last day, the great day of the feast, Jesus stood and cried, saying, If any man thirst, let him come unto Me, and drink. He that believeth on Me, as the Scripture hath said, out of his belly shall flow rivers of living water. (But this spake He of the Spirit, which they that believe on Him should receive: for the Holy Ghost was not yet given; because that Jesus was not yet glorified.)'*

As the water was being poured out of earthen vessels on the last great day of the feast, Jesus stood and loudly said, 'If any man thirst, let him come unto Me, and drink.' Here are three necessary requirements.
1.   A man, any man, must sense and become acutely aware of his need for spiritual water. This desire must be as real to him spiritually as thirst is

physically. The reason many do not drink is they have no true desire for the Spirit.

2. A man must come to Jesus as the source of all spiritual blessings. Only through Jesus can one drink of the Spirit which proceeds from the Father.

3. The believer must drink. None drinks with his mouth closed, and this is likewise true in the spiritual realm. This involves asking. Jesus said,

> '...*how much more shall your heavenly Father give the Holy Spirit to them that ask Him?*'
> (Luke 11:13)

One must open his mouth wide believing God to fill it (see Psalm 81:10).

We drink of the supernatural Spirit flowing from the supernatural Savior with a supernatural utterance. It is here that the value of tongues comes into focus. The believer is 'made to drink into one Spirit' by speaking in other tongues (see 1 Corinthians 12:13).

John 7:38 shows the ministry of the believer after his thirst has been quenched by drinking to the full of the living water:

> '*He that believeth on Me, as the Scripture hath said, out of his belly* (the believer's spirit) *shall flow rivers of living water.*'

It is important to note that although the believer has a release of the Spirit from within, Christ Himself is the only individual who actually had water flowing out of His belly as did the wilderness rock. Some commentators read verse 38 this way:

> *'He that believes on Me (**may drink from Me**), as the Scripture hath said, Out of His belly* (the Rock's) *shall flow rivers of living water.'*

They take it to mean that *his belly* is Christ's, not the believer's. We can partially accept this view as a believer has nothing to flow from his spirit while in a thirsty state and that only by drinking from that which flows from Christ is the believer able to in turn minister the same to others.

The belly corresponds to the believer's spirit. Out of the regenerated, refreshed human spirit flows the Holy Spirit. This is outflow. Outflow is determined from inflow which is the Holy Spirit's flow into the believer's spirit, *'proceeding out of the throne of God and of the Lamb'* (Revelation 22:1).

A believer's rate of inflow is determined by the frequency and amount of the Spirit he drinks from the Rock as he speaks loving words of praise to Christ. Thus we can observe that the believer's ministry to others is dependent upon his fellowship with Christ.

> *'A man can receive nothing except it be given him from heaven.'*   (John 3:27)

We can minister nothing except that which we have received. Drinking is determined by speaking, as can be seen in the Lord's instruction to Moses, *'speak ye unto the rock'* (Numbers 20:8). We are to *'be **being** filled'* (literal Greek) with the Spirit speaking to ourselves in psalms, hymns, and spiritual songs (see Ephesians 5:18–19). Realizing that Jesus has been smitten once forevermore to reign as King of kings and Lord of lords we can speak to the glorified Christ at the Father's right hand and drink to the full abundantly.

That there can be no doubt this living water is the Holy Spirit is seen in John's note of explanation given in parentheses in John 7:39.

> *'(But this spake He of the Spirit, which they that believe on Him should receive: for the Holy Ghost was not yet given; because that Jesus was not yet glorified.)'*

Believers should receive the Holy Spirit for believing involves receiving.

> *'Have ye received the Holy Ghost since ye believed?'*
> (Acts 19:2)

Jesus has been glorified and the Holy Ghost has been given. Are you drinking daily of the Spirit?

> *'... the Holy Ghost came on them; and they spake with tongues...'* (Acts 19:6)

If we truly believe Christ we will want all that He has for us.

Notice John's statement in John 19:34: *'... forthwith came there out Blood and Water.'* Some believe the Blood flowed with the Water in two separate, but simultaneously flowing streams. Others believe that the Blood flowed first and then Water began flowing. I prefer the latter opinion for one must first be cleansed by the blood of Jesus before he can receive the baptism with the Holy Spirit. [3] Jesus said,

> *'Even the Spirit of truth whom the world cannot receive.'* (John 14:17)

The smitten rock and the death of Christ both resulted in outpourings of water. The water Israel drank refreshed them so that they were able to win a battle with Amalek shortly afterward (see Exodus 17:8).[4] The living water (the Holy Spirit) strengthens and refreshes the believer, making him victorious over the enemy.

Paul adds that the wilderness Rock followed Israel. That the literal boulder rolled alongside the Israelites is not the intended meaning. The 'spiritual Rock' who was Christ, as the Angel of the Lord followed or led Israel, throughout their wilderness experience. It was this angel with whom Moses spoke face to face.

Jesus accompanies the sojourning believer in all the earthly pilgrimage as the strong rock of defense and spiritual refreshing.

> *'Lo, I am with you always, even unto the end of the world.'* (Matthew 28:20)

> *'...for He hath said, I will never leave thee nor forsake thee. So that we may boldly say, The Lord is my helper, and I will not fear what man shall do unto me.'* (Hebrews 13:5–6)

He is always with us, and as our Rock we may speak unto Him in all situations of life, no matter what crisis arrives, and drink freely of the water of life that only He can give.

When a Christian rejects the fullness of the Spirit he is telling Jesus, 'Not all that you accomplished in my

behalf do I accept or appreciate.' Let's accept everything Jesus has provided for us.

> *'To shew that the* LORD *is upright: He is my rock,*
> *and there is no unrighteousness in Him.'*

(Psalm 92:15)

Additional Notes

1. Authorities estimate the population anywhere from 600,000 to
   12,000,000! Most agree, however, with two to three million at the
   time of the Exodus.
2. Moses succumbed to the same temptation many men of God fall
   prey to: he felt he and Aaron 'fetch(ed) you water' rather than
   realizing that it was God's sole responsibility.
3. The Blood and Water must have another meaning as well. The first
   woman was taken from Adam's fleshly side while he slept. The
   'last Adam' was dead when His side was opened. The Blood that
   flowed from His side made us joint-heirs who are seated with Him.
   The Water typifies the application, by the Holy Spirit, of the Word
   of God to believers – making them His corporate Bride (see Ephesians 5:26ff). 'The marriage of the Lamb is come, and His wife
   hath made herself ready.'
4. Amalek, Esau's seed, typifies the flesh nature we must deal with
   after we have been saved. 'The battle with Amalek is from generation to generation' (our flesh battles are continued and frequent)
   until 'I will utterly blot out the remembrance of Amalek from
   under heaven.'

Questions on Chapter 12

1. On the first occasion of bringing water out of the
    rock, Moses struck the rock as God commanded
    him. What did he do wrong on the second
    occasion?

    _____

    _____

    What should he have done instead?

    _____

    _____

2. In what respect was the rock Israel drank from a
    picture of Christ?

    _____

    _____

3. Give at least three parallels between the rock in
    the wilderness and the Rock on the cross:

    _____

    _____

    _____

4. What is the significance of speaking to the Rock?

    _____

    _____

    _____

5. What was the water that flowed from His smitten
    side a picture of?

    _____

6. How do we drink this living water today?

    _____

    _____

    _____

Appendix

Modern Errors Concerning the Blood

In our final remarks we are obligated to an unpleasant task: identify and reprove common errors presently circulating concerning the blood of Christ. The Word of God is given to us, not only for edification and instruction, but also for reproof and correction:

> *'All scripture is given by the inspiration of God and is profitable for doctrine, for reproof, for correction, for instruction in righteousness: That the man of God may be perfect, thoroughly furnished unto all good works.'*　　　　(2 Timothy 3:16–17)

> *'These things speak, and exhort, and rebuke with all authority. Let no man despise thee.'*　　　(Titus 2:15)

With this in mind let us proceed to a few of the more common errors...

David and Jonathan Cut Themselves

One of the most touching scenes of human friendship in the Bible is contained in the story of David and

Jonathan. Their unselfish love caused Jonathan to love David *'as his own soul'* and moved David, at news of Jonathan's death to exclaim:

> *'I am distressed for you, my brother Jonathan; You have been very pleasant to me;* **Your love to me was wonderful** *surpassing the love of women.'*
>
> (2 Samuel 1:26)

Let's read about the love covenant these godly men made:

> *'And it was so, when he had finished speaking to Saul, that the soul of Jonathan was knit to the soul of David, and Jonathan loved him as his own soul. ... Then Jonathan and David made a covenant, because he loved him as his own soul. And Jonathan took off the robe that was on him and gave it to David, with his armor, even to his sword and his bow and his belt.'* (1 Samuel 18:1, 3, 4)

> *' "And you shall not only show me the kindness of the LORD while I still live, that I may not die; but you shall not cut off your kindness from my house forever, no, not when the LORD has cut off every one of the enemies of David from the face of the earth." So Jonathan made a covenant with the house of David, saying, "Let the LORD require it at the hand of David's enemies." And Jonathan again caused David to vow, because he loved him; for he loved him as he loved his own soul.'* (1 Samuel 20:14–17)

The error sometimes heard is that these two friends, when making this covenant with each other, supposedly cut their wrists, dripped the blood into a goblet, mixed their blood with wine, and drank the mixture in order to seal the covenant.

One well-known teacher produced a book all about this covenant. On the cover of the book the artist shows two men joining their wrists together while their blood drops into the goblet below. In the background a holy man, perhaps Samuel, stands as a solemn witness to the proceedings. Throughout the book phrases hinting at the supposed event appear.

It is sad that this error is so greatly promoted in this particular book, as there is much truth in it. I wrote this minister several years ago with the information I present to you below. No reply ever came (his staff probably never gave it to him), and to the best of my knowledge, this book is still being distributed.

Yesterday I took a break from writing to go over some of the mail. A magazine, which I always enjoy, had an article by a brother who serves on their ministry staff. Once again there was much valid information in his article, for which I was grateful. But right in the middle of his teaching on David and Jonathan he said they may have 'cut themselves or an animal' when they made their covenant. By suggesting the possibility of mutilation, many readers may be misled into accepting such at face value. [1]

So what?

First, in Deuteronomy 14:1 we see Yahweh's prohibiting any cutting of the skin to the whole nation of Israel: [2]

> '*Ye are the children of the* LORD *your God: ye shall not cut yourselves . . .* '

The only exception to this commandment was another commandment given many times to Abraham and his descendants: *circumcision*. Mutilation of any kind was strictly forbidden.

David and Jonathan, who were devoted to the pure worship of their God, would never have cut their wrists, knowing,

> *'For thou art an holy people unto the* LORD *thy God, and the* LORD *hath chosen thee to be a peculiar people unto Himself, above all the nations that are upon the earth.'* (Deuteronomy 14:2)

The people of other nations did cut themselves in making covenants; but not God's chosen people.

The word 'covenant' in 1 Samuel 18:3 is *berith* and does mean 'to cut' (as we studied in chapter 10). What then was cut? No doubt, an animal was halved between the two men. This then made them 'blood brothers', so to speak, and not a slice in the wrist.

Second, Jonathan and David would have never drunk blood of any kind. They knew the often repeated prohibition from eating any manner of blood whatsoever:

> *'But you shall not eat flesh with its life, that is, its blood.'* (Genesis 9:4)

> *'This shall be a perpetual statute throughout your generations in all your dwellings: you shall eat neither fat nor blood.'* (Leviticus 3:17)

> *'Moreover you shall not eat any blood in any of your dwellings, whether of bird of beast.'*
>
> (Leviticus 7:26)

> *'And whatever man of the house of Israel, or of the strangers who sojourn among you, who eats any blood, I will set My face against that person who eats blood, and will cut him off from among his people.'*　　　　　　(Leviticus 17:10)

> *'You shall not eat anything with the blood...'*
> 　　　　　　(Leviticus 19:26)

Let's look at only one more commandment which David himself remembered and observed in a most unique manner:

> *'However, you may slaughter and eat meat within all your gates, whatever your heart desires, according to the blessing of the LORD your God which He has given you. .... **Only you shall not eat the blood; you shall pour it on the earth like water.**'*
> 　　　　　　(Deuteronomy 12:15–16)

Now, compare this commandment (to pour out blood upon the ground as water) to an event in one of David's military campaigns against the Philistines:

> *'And David said with longing, "Oh, that someone would give me a drink of the water from the well of Bethlehem, which is by the gate!" So the three mighty men broke through the camp of the Philistines, drew water from the well of Bethlehem that was by the gate, and took it and brought it to David. **Nevertheless he would not drink it, but poured it out to the LORD.** And he said, "Far be it from me, O LORD, that I should do this! **Is this not the blood of the men** who went in jeopardy of their lives?" Therefore he would not drink it.'*　　(2 Samuel 23:15–17)

The modern error that David and Jonathan mingled their blood together with wine and drank it has been propagated by **no fewer than 15 Bible teachers** throughout the Body of Christ. *'Dead flies cause the ointment of the apothecary to send forth a stinking savor: so doth a little folly him that is in reputation for wisdom and honor'* (Ecclesiastes 10:1). Surely this error is a 'dead fly' in the fragrant ointment of the Jonathan and David covenant.

The fact is, as is widely documented, that peoples throughout history have cut their wrists and have drunk a little blood in solemnizing oaths and covenants with each other. **This was strictly forbidden in Israel** and would not have been allowed by two godly men like David and Jonathan (see Deuteronomy 18:9–14). Think of the injustice we are doing to David and Jonathan when we teach, or even permit, **a common witchcraft practice** to be spoken concerning them!

The only blood of man that God required in Israel was the blood of circumcision. In essence, the Hebrew was giving God his personal blood (life) at the very source of paternity, pledging both himself and those who would come after him in the line of natural descent, to Yahweh alone. All other cuttings of the flesh were considered *'abominations unto the* LORD*'* (Deuteronomy 18:10–12).

Ordinary Blood

Some ministers and theologians teach that the blood of Jesus was ordinary blood, like yours and mine. They use Hebrews 2:14 to substantiate their view:

> *'Forasmuch then as the children are partakers of flesh and blood, He also Himself likewise took part of the same . . .'*

The often heard comment goes like this: 'Since He partook of **the same** flesh and blood as ours it follows that there is no difference between them.'

In his comment on this verse, A.B. Bruce pointed out:

> 'The difficulty arises in part from our trying to put too much theology into the passage.'
>
> (*The Epistle to the Hebrews*, p. 119)

Indeed.

Especially when we consider that the writer did not use *koinonia* (to share fully in), but *metechos* (to take part but not all). Even as the King James renders it *'He . . . took part of the same'* rather than 'He . . . **took all** of the same'.

Jesus 'took part', but not all, of the same flesh and blood we have when He identified with us in becoming a Man. That He did not take the sinful part of us in the Incarnation is clearly evident.[3] Consider the following scriptures with me.

Acts 2:27

David spoke of Jesus in Psalm 16 which Peter quoted in Acts 2:24–28. Verse 27 says,

> *'Because Thou wilt not leave My soul in hell* (hades), *neither wilt Thou suffer Thine Holy One to see corruption.'*

The body of Jesus laid in the tomb three days and nights. When Lazarus had been dead only one day longer, his sister said, *'by this time he stinketh'* (John 11:39).

Does it not then follow that the physical body of our Savior should have begun to decay shortly after He died, as with the physical bodies of all 'ordinary' people? Further proof is that Jesus was not embalmed, only wrapped in clean linen (see Matthew 27:59; Mark 15:46; Luke 23:53). Corruption should have begun at once, but 72 hours later, the body in the tomb had not experienced any decay whatsoever!

Although Jesus came *'in the likeness of sinful flesh'* we must remember that *'in Him is no sin'* (Romans 8:3; 1 John 3:5). He came *'in the likeness'* of sinful man in that He was born a man with all of man's characteristics **except sin**. He was *'without sin'* and *'knew no sin'* (Hebrews 4:15; 2 Corinthians 5:21). This was the purpose of the virgin birth ... He was born without original sin, or the carnal sin nature of Adam. He was a man, but He was **a perfect man**.

In Acts 2:27 Jesus is referred to as God's *'Holy One'* whom God would not permit to see corruption. This is one more example of the fact of **legal imputation** of our sin at Calvary.

1 Peter 1:18–19

Another text which disproves the fallacy that Jesus' blood was ordinary is this foundational scripture:

> *'Forasmuch as ye know that ye were not redeemed with corruptible things, as silver and gold, ... But with the precious blood of Christ, as of a lamb without blemish and without spot.'*

Notice that Peter clearly says we are not redeemed *'with corruptible things ... but with the precious blood of Christ ...'*

The Blood, then, is **incorruptible**.

I was exceeding blessed reading in Zodhiates' *Lexical Aids To The New Testament* the following definition of *phthartos*, which is the Greek word Peter used for 'corruptible'. Remember, the following definition tells us what the blood of Christ is **not**:

> 'to corrupt, corruptible, the essential quality of the body of man, equivalent to *thnetos*, mortal ... used to indicate degenerate man ... *ptheiro*; to corrupt, destroy ... to corrupt, spoil, vitiate, in a moral or spiritual sense...'

This definition teaches that the precious blood of Christ was and is not 'corruptible' both in a moral and spiritual sense! **Hallelujah!**

You see, dear friend, when Adam ate of the fruit of the tree of knowledge of good and evil he was 'blood poisoned'.Sin is inherent in the genes and chromosomes of man, passed on through the blood line of our ancestry.

> '...*by one man's disobedience many were made sinners ... in Adam all die.*'
>
> (Romans 5:19; 1 Corinthians 15:22)

All men, whether black, yellow, brown, white, or red are made of *'one blood'* (Acts 17:26). And all men sin and die.

Most diseases are directly traceable to the blood, confirming that 'the life' indeed 'is in the blood' (Leviticus 17:11). Through the sin of our first parents we were all born under the dominion of death.

But Jesus was, in this sense, different from us. His body was conceived apart from the seed of man, supernaturally conceived by the Holy Ghost. When He was born into this world He was called *'that holy thing'* (Luke 1:35). Mary's egg was not fertilized by the Holy Spirit, no, a thousand times **No!**

His body was entirely prepared by God in the virgin's womb. Hebrews 10:5 bears this out also: *'a body hast Thou prepared Me.'*

H.A. Maxwell White points out in *The Power of the Blood,* 'Mary was the chosen carrier of the body...' But the body itself and the blood that flowed in it were entirely made by the creative power of God. The Incarnation was a miracle!

Someone would object saying that His temptations would not be real to Him as ours are real to us, forgetting the fact that the first man, Adam, was created totally sinless and pure, too.

The blood that flowed in Jesus' body was pure blood, holy blood, innocent blood, living blood, and precious (rare) blood! It was and is **incorruptible blood** – not subject to moral or spiritual degeneration.

No wonder Beelzebub (lord of the flies) hates this precious blood so! It is the opposite of everything he is and he, the corruptible one, cannot touch it! Like flies in nature, however, our mortal corruptible blood has been swarmed over in our spiritual death. There is deliverance in Jesus, as prophesied in Joel:

> *'And I will cleanse their blood ... for the LORD dwelleth in Zion.'*　　　　　　　　(Joel 3:21)

It is, no doubt, incorrect to sing 'His royal blood now flows in my veins' as we still bear *'the image of the earthy'* (1 Corinthians 15:49). Rather, His precious blood has *'purged our conscience from dead works'* and gives us boldness *'to enter the holiest of all'* (Hebrews 9:14, 10:19). This Blood transfusion occurs in the spiritual realm, imparting eternal life, because *'the life is in the blood.'*

Acts 20:28

Paul instructed the Ephesian elders *'to feed the church of God, which He hath purchased with His own blood.'* The second person of the Godhead is not specifically named in Acts 20:24–34. *'His own blood'* can only refer, in this verse to none other than God Himself, our Father. Inasmuch as He is Spirit (John 4:24) and not physical we must pray for illumination on this phrase: *'the church of God which He hath purchased with His own blood'* receiving almost at once the crystal clear understanding that this phrase refers to the blood of Emmanuel and that it was blood entirely manufactured by the Father. Hence, *'His own blood'* through which God purchased the Church out of the world in Christ.

Pleading the Blood

I don't suppose I will ever forget my first experience with 'pleading the Blood' as it was called. I was only a few months old in the Lord and was present at a small prayer meeting. A dear older saint began chanting 'the Blood ... the Blood ... the Blood ... the Blood ... the Blood' for a period of 10 or 15 minutes without cessation. Although I was quite young in the Lord I knew deep inside that what she was doing was wrong.

In fact, she seemed to have a superstitious air about her, almost a self-induced, trance-like state. It reminded me of 'mantra chanting' done by the yogis I had associated with before conversion, which I myself had done 'while in meditation'.

A few years later, after several more encounters with 'pleading the Blood' by several sincere Christians, I did a Scripture search in regards to this practice. I found:

1. Not even one example of so-called 'pleading the Blood' by early Christians;

2. Not even one scripture which referred to 'pleading the Blood';

3. A reproof of 'vain repetitions' by Jesus Himself (Matthew 6:7);

4. The closest thing I found to 'pleading the Blood' was the reference in Hebrews 12:24 which says *'the blood of sprinkling that speaketh better things than that of Abel.'* Hence, it is the Blood that does indeed speak, even from the mercy-seat in heaven, as we have previously seen in this book.

I also noticed that this practice of 'pleading the Blood' was observed most often during the casting out of evil spirits in a classical pentecostal environment. When questioning those who 'pled the Blood' afterwards I discovered the 'pleaders' were afraid of the possible attack of exorcised evil spirits and that by 'pleading the Blood' the demons would be warded off from attacking the 'pleaders'.

It is easy to notice, however, that Philip did not instruct those in attendance at his city-wide meetings in Samaria to 'plead the Blood' and it is said that *'unclean spirits, crying with loud voice, came out of many that were possessed with them'* (Acts 8:7).

This practice, which is at least extra-biblical, is based on **superstitious fear** which 2 Timothy 1:7 clearly teaches is not from God.

Furthermore, we are specifically instructed to use the **Name** of Jesus, rather than the **Blood** of Jesus, when casting out demons (see Mark 16:17; Luke 10:17; Acts 16:18).

Those who attempt to justify 'pleading the Blood' on the basis of Revelation 12:11 are guilty of aberration. That verse does indeed teach the value of making vocal affirmations (the meaning of *'the word of their testimony'*) of the merits of Christ's blood, and thereby overcoming the accuser (Satan). This would be confessing specific merits of the Blood when in mental battle with the enemy, not a monotonous repetition of 'the Blood ... the Blood ... the Blood' as an enchantment against the devil. In fact, Deuteronomy 18:10 refers to *'an enchanter'* as *'an abomination unto the LORD'* (Deuteronomy 18:12).

The precious blood of Jesus is definitely supernatural, but in no way is it magical or mystical. We should reprove, in love, those who engage in this unscriptural practice, showing them instead the value of confessing various merits of the Blood as we studied earlier in this book.

Example: 'Because the Word of God says the blood of Jesus is holy, I am holy by the precious blood' (see Hebrews 13:12; 1 John 1:7). This type of confession can defeat the accuser of the brethren when he assaults our minds with condemnation.

> *'And they overcame him* (the accuser) *by the blood of the Lamb, and by the word of their testimony; and they loved not their lives unto the death.'*
>
> (Revelation 12:11)

See pages 108, 109, 166–174.

Receive with joy the revelation of the Blood! The Holy Spirit Himself will guide you into this precious truth of Scripture.

All that you have read in this book is but a beginning; not an exhaustive conclusion. This book is meant to serve only as a guide to a deeper and fuller under-standing of the Blood.

I trust you have gained something more from the Lord through this study.

Additional Notes

1. I later wrote the writer of this article and received a prompt reply that he was dismayed over the editor's mistake in his article and that he did not believe David and Jonathan cut themselves in any fashion. Nevertheless, thousands read it.

2. God had previously given the same commandment for the priest-hood: *'They shall not ... make any cuttings in their flesh. They shall be holy unto their God, and not profane the name of their God'* (Leviticus 21:5–6).

3. To dispute the fact of sovereign creatorship of the Messiah's body some have quoted Galatians 4:4, *'God sent forth His Son, made of a woman ... '* The word 'made' used here is the Greek word *ginomai* and it better rendered 'born' rather than 'made' as it means 'to come into existence'; i.e., the birth of our Savior brought Him into our existence with us. W.E. Vine and most other scholars agree that *ginomai* means 'born' both times it appears in Galatians 4:4 *'born of a woman, born under the Law.'* Jesus was *'the seed of the woman'* (Genesis 3:15) in that He was her offspring.

A Final Word

Let God show you the special sacredness of the Blood. He views all blood as sacred – even animal blood was commanded to be poured on the ground and covered with dust by the hunter who procured its meat for food.

Man's blood is even more sacred – because he was made in the image of God. His blood, when unjustly shed, can only be revenged by the murderer's blood.

Jesus' blood, however, holds the chief place of dearness in the heart of God. Because Jesus was who He was and lived as He lived, the blood He poured out on the ground (epitomizing all that He is) is worthy of special veneration by God and man.

John's vision into the heavenlies revealed great congregations worshiping Jesus in His great role of Redeemer. (Repeatedly we behold *the Lamb who had been slain'* who *'redeemed us to God by "His" blood.'* Their robes had been *'washed and made white'* in the Lamb's blood making them worthy to stand *'before the throne of God.'*)

Have you experienced the saving power of Jesus Christ?

If not, you can be assured that Jesus died for **you** when He *'tasted death for every man.'* His blood made the propitiation for your sins.

Call on Him today!

> *'For whosoever shall call upon the name of the Lord shall be saved.'* (Romans 10:13)

If you have been so washed may you *'give unto the Lord the glory due unto His name'* and may you never listen to the father of lies who would urge you to count *'the blood of the covenant'* as *'an unholy thing.'* Those who do this trample the Son of God under their feet! No wonder, then, that they are worthy of a *'sorer punishment'* than mere physical execution.

Multitudes of Christians are ignorant of the great value God attaches to the blood of Jesus. Many ministers speak of the precious blood of Christ in an almost apologetic tone!

You have seen in this study guide why the Blood makes atonement and covenant a living, reality between God and man.

Answers to Questions

Chapter 1

1. The concept of sacrifice means, to most believers, to give up something of value, or endure something of hardness for the Lord.
2. David realized that a sacrifice which cost the sacrificer nothing is not a sacrifice.
3. Solomon's costly sacrifice at the dedication of the Temple foreshadowed the costly expense God's Lamb required of Him. Salvation is not cheap.
4. Valuable, costly, honorable, highly esteemed, beloved, held as of great price, held in honor, especially dear.
5. The blood that flowed in Jesus' body was supernaturally created by God the Father who purchased the Church with His blood (Acts 20:28).
6. Paul and Peter both said that Jesus purchased us from the slave market of sin with His precious blood.
7. Give whatever the blood of Christ means to you in this answer, then come back at the conclusion of the book and review your answer. If you can answer much more then than you can now, this book was worth your time investment.

Chapter 2

1. They were probably clothed with light garments even as God has so clothed Himself.

2.	Immediately after they partook of the forbidden fruit.
3.	To hide the shame of their nakedness.
4.	To typify the robe of righteousness He would clothe repentant sinners with in the day of salvation.
5.	Animal skins.
6.	He evidently slew innocent animals to provide a covering for guilty man.
7.	(a) God requires the shedding of blood for sin; (b) the sinner must be covered by the blood; (c) God provided the sacrifice; (d) God covers the sinner with the blood; (e) the innocent dies for the guilty; (f) God brings judgment on the sacrifice.
8.	That children learned much from an early age concerning blood sacrifice long before the Law was given by Moses.
9.	Yes, fathers especially should bring up children in the nurture and admonition of the Lord according to Ephesians 6:4.

Chapter 3

1.	By telling ministers the Blood message is socially unattractive; by saying that the shedding of blood was not central to redemption – just the death of Christ in whatever fashion was needful.
2.	Cain's offering of the fruit of the ground.
3.	Yes, the phrasing of Scripture in Genesis 4:1 implies that Eve conceived once and bore twice. If this is not the case, they were relatively close in age because they were both full grown adults involved in their livelihoods when the incident occurred.
4.	He believed the word of his parents and faith came by hearing. It was not that Abel had more faith than Cain, period, but that he had faith in the message he heard and by faith offered a more excellent sacrifice than Cain.
5.	Yes, it was willful rejection on his part.
6.	The Lord gave Cain a second chance to bring a sacrifice in Genesis 4:7a. He warned Cain that a bad attitude would result in a bad action if left unchecked in Genesis

4:7b. After banishing Cain *'from the presence of the LORD'* (Genesis 4:16) God showed mercy in that He spoke a promise of vengeance on anyone who took his life and gave him a protective mark in Genesis 4:15.

7. Involuntary, clearly supernatural, visible witness apart from human involvement, probably fire.

8. No, John taught that Cain's works were evil and that his motivation was competition, envy, and hatred in 1 John 3:11–15.

9. The wicked one.

10. In 1 John 3:12 the Word says, *'. . . and his brother's* (Abel's) *righteous'* (meaning Abel's sacrificial firstlings).

11. Religion. Cain ended up shedding blood, after all, but incurred divine disfavor because his brother was righteous (by faith).

12. Eternal rejection from the presence of God (see Genesis 4:12–16).

13. Yes, the blood of Abel spoke out to the Lord for vengeance from the ground it soaked in Genesis 4:10. The life principle is in the blood (Leviticus 17:11) and because life was unjustly taken, the dying life called out to the Creator of life for retribution. Jesus referred to Abel's blood in Matthew 23:35 and Luke 11:51.

14. The Scripture implies it cries out for mercy and life for the transgressor in Hebrews 12:24.

Chapter 4

1. Thirty-three times. At the same age He became the lamb sacrifice for sinners.

2. He fulfilled each levitical requirement concerning lamb sacrifice. Briefly, He was perfect (without spot or blemish), He was offered as a sin offering, He was slain, and He was a lamb for the whole race of man.

3. Yes, His body was formed by the Holy Spirit and because He lived without sin, the forerunner of death (sickness) had no claim on Him.

4. At the Jordan John saw Jesus coming and declared, *'Behold the lamb of God which takes away the sin of the world'* (John 1:29).
5. In Genesis there was a lamb offered for a man. In Exodus a lamb was offered for the family. In Leviticus a lamb was offered for the nation of Israel. Jesus is our personal redeemer, if we believe on Him our family can be saved. He will heal our land if we turn to Him. Finally, He became the fullest application of the lamb sacrifice: a Lamb for the world!

Chapter 5

1. The plague was called 'the death of the firstborn'.
2. The passover lamb was 'a lamb for an house' and corresponds to Acts 16:31. If the household was too little, the lamb was to be shared with the neighbor next door – we are to share Jesus from 'house to house'. The passover lamb was to be 'without blemish' as Peter affirms Christ was 'without spot'. The passover lamb was killed in the evening corresponding to the supernatural darkness that hung over all the land the final three hours of the crucifixion. The paschal lamb's blood was not to be applied to the threshold of the door – Jesus' blood is not to be trampled underfoot. The bread and lamb meat signified the body and blood of our Lord. The infirm Hebrews were made healthy eating the passover meal and enabled to walk for many hours to the Red Sea.
3. Yes. Luke 23:44–45 states, *'There was a darkness over all the earth ... And the sun was darkened ... '*
4. Yes. 'A much sorer punishment' than physical death awaits the apostate (Hebrews 10:28–29).
5. Leaven typifies iniquity, false doctrine, hypocrisy, uncleanness, and legalism.
6. We are to partake of Christ with the 'unleavened bread of sincerity and truth' (1 Corinthians 5:8). To feast on Jesus, our Passover Lamb, we must depart from iniquity.

7. In the sense that they were to partake of Him spiritually and in reality. It was a figure of speech common at the time.
8. Fire represents judgment which fell on Jesus on the cross. If it were boiled, they would be, in effect, watering down the Gospel.
9. No. The destroyer.
10. The word 'token' means 'evidence, sign' and refers to the fact that our testimony of the blood is a sign of our redemption.
11. John said we are to 'abide in Him; that when He shall appear, we may have confidence, and not be ashamed before Him at His coming' (1 John 2:28).
12. No. Neither can we see the blood that covers us, for 'we walk by faith, not by sight' (2 Corinthians 5:7).

Chapter 6

1. Our justification is based upon the blood of Christ.
2. The levitical laws provide a shadow (outline) of good things to come in Christ.
3. The cleansing of the leper perfectly foreshadows justification by the blood of Christ.
4. Sin. Leviticus 13:44–46; Numbers 12:8–16; 2 Chronicles 26:16–23. Criticism of His leader, exaltation in pride.
5. Yes.
6. No. Obedience without understanding.
7. One day. The initial salvation experience (justification and regeneration).
8. They had to be **alive** and **clean**.
9. The crucifixion and resurrection of Jesus Christ.
10. The cross.
11. The atonement.
12. Faith.
13. Yes (Revelation 12:11) by our vocal agreement.
14. The human body of our Savior.
15. The 'eternal Spirit' who offered His sacrifice.
16. To picture complete and total cleansing.

17. The resurrected Savior who carried His blood into the heavenly holy place.

Chapter 7

1. Leviticus 14:14–18 primarily foreshadow the work of sanctification by the blood of Christ and the anointings that result from the work of sanctification.
2. The seven days elapsing between the initial cleansing and the second cleansing picture a desire for perfection in the heart of the believer.
3. The return to the camp after the period of alienation due to leprosy pictures reconciliation with God and with His people.
4. The water bath following the blood cleansing pictures the truth of 'the washing of water by the Word' so vital after conversion.
5. On the eighth day he goes to the priest at the door of the tabernacle and offers sacrifice to the Lord consisting of two male lambs (for a sin offering and for a trespass offering) and an ewe lamb for a burnt offering. A log of oil is waved before the Lord.
6. The priest takes some of the blood of the lamb which was offered as a trespass offering and puts it upon the tip of the right ear, upon the thumb of the right hand, and upon the big toe of the right foot.
7. The blood was applied to the right side because that direction speaks of divine favor throughout the Bible (see Matthew 25:33; Mark 16:19; John 21:6; Revelation 1:17).
8. The five principal areas of the Lamb's body opened for us were:
    (a) the back
    (b) the head
    (c) the hands
    (d) the feet
    (e) the side
9. The corresponding significance in the believer's life is:
    (a) healing and physical health by Jesus' stripes

216

(b) holy thoughts and the exchange/renewal of the mind of Christ

(c) the works and ministry of Christ reproduced in the believer

(d) the believer's walk and fellowship

(e) the believer's position and heirship

10. Jesus never had an evil thought because He said, 'Evil thoughts defile' (Mark 7:20–23) a person and He was 'undefiled' (Hebrews 7:26).

11. A Christian can silence the voice of the accuser of the brethren by vocally claiming the merits of Christ's blood.

12. Yes. On the basis of applying the blood to the earlobe, we see scriptural support for a believer claiming divine help for his or her thought life. The blood of Christ provides the legal basis for victory in the believer's thought life.

13. The believer's hands represent his works or ministry, warfare, and healing ministry.

14. The term 'walk' in 1 John 1:7 represents the believer's fellowship with God and with the other saints. The blood signifies cleansing for fellowship.

15. The oil represents the anointing of the Holy Spirit. The blood is the legal basis of authority; the Holy Spirit gives the actual empowering. Therefore, the oil had to be applied after and upon the blood because the Spirit answers to the blood of Christ today.

16. Yes, a Christian may easily chart his or her progress according to the outline in Leviticus 14:1–18. I am presently in verses 14–17 greatly desiring verse 18!

Chapter 8

1. Jesus Christ is the focal object of the Word of God. The reason is He is the One of whom the prophets spoke, and He alone fulfilled all their prophecies.

2. Zechariah foresaw Christ as 'a fountain opened' when He would make the supreme sacrifice 'for sin and for uncleanness.'

3. One day.

4. Jesus Christ was a fountain sealed until the day His skin was pierced. When the skin of His body was punctured, the fountain was opened.
5. No. Isaiah 50:6
6. Because He had already died, the Roman soldiers did not break the legs of Christ (Exodus 12:46; Psalm 34:20).
7. Acts 2:23, 15:18; Hebrews 4:3; Revelation 13:8.
8. Yes. Isaiah 50:6–7, 52:14, 53; Psalm 22:16; Deuteronomy 21:23; Zechariah 13:6; and many others.

Chapter 9

1. Yes. In chapters 1 and 42.
2. Hedge.
3. Job's person, Job's house and family, Job's possessions, Job's endeavors, and Job's influence.
4. Yes. Ecclesiastes 10:8.
5. Acts 16:31.
6. Job prayed for his friends and God turned his captivity.
7. Twice as much.
8. No. Job did actually have 14 sons and 6 daughters. The first half were in Paradise and the second half were born to him in the restoration of 'twice as much'.

Chapter 10

1. 'To cut; to cut asunder'
2. The Greek word *diatheke* means 'a testament or will'.
3. Yes. Abimelech and Isaac, Jacob and Laban, David and Jonathan.
4. No. They halved a prized animal from each of their flocks.
5. Eight.
6. Noah, Abraham, David, Hezekiah, Jehoida, Josiah.
7. The New Covenant is in His blood (the blood of Jesus).
8. Book/people.
9. Three.
10. Blood.
11. 1 Peter 1:2.

12. Daily and boldly. We may enter on the basis of the Blood.
13. 60.
14. No. He entered the Holiest of All in heaven itself.
15. Forgiveness, holiness, healing, infilling of the Holy Spirit.
16. Because his name is not written in heaven. This is the basis of relationship with God which entitles us to the authority of the Name of Jesus as believers.
17. True.
18. False.
19. True.
20. False.
21. True.
22. False.

Chapter 11

1. At least 25 descriptive adjectives of the Blood are as follows:
    (1) Justifying (Romans 5:9)
    (2) Redeeming (Revelation 5:9)
    (3) Remitting (Hebrews 9:22)
    (4) Forgiving (Ephesians 1:7)
    (5) Washing and freeing (Revelation 1:5)
    (6) Purging (Hebrews 9:14)
    (7) Cleansing (1 John 1:7)
    (8) Sanctifying (Hebrews 13:12)
    (9) Reconciling (Ephesians 2:13)
    (10) Blotting (Colossians 2:14)
    (11) Triumphing (Colossians 2:15)
    (12) Overcoming (Revelation 12:11)
    (13) Agreeing (1 John 5:8)
    (14) Communing (1 Corinthians 10:16)
    (15) Purchasing (Acts 20:28)
    (16) Sprinkling (Hebrews 12:24)
    (17) Speaking (Hebrews 12:24)
    (18) Incorruptible (1 Peter 1:18)
    (19) Precious (1 Peter 1:19)

(20) Holy (Hebrews 10:29)
(21) Atoning (Leviticus 17:11)
(22) Innocent (Matthew 27:4)
(23) Accessing (Hebrews 10:19)
(24) Perfect (John 19:30)
(25) Sheltering (Exodus 12:23)

Others are:

(26) Shed (Luke 22:20)
(27) Saving (Zechariah 9:11)
(28) Whitening (Revelation 7:14–15)
(29) Peacemaking (Colossians 1:20)

2. We can overcome the accuser of the brethren by the merit of Jesus' blood and our vocal agreement with it as we fully commit our lives to God.
3. Confessed sin is: blotted out, forgotten, removed, plunged out of sight, and cast behind God's back.

Chapter 12

1. Moses struck the rock twice on the second occasion. He should have taken his rod (symbolic of authority) and only spoken to the rock, but not hit it at all.
2. That Messiah would be smitten, as was the rock at Horeb in Exodus 17:6, and that He would provide living water for thirsty believers as a result of that smiting.
3. **Wilderness rock**
    (a) was non-living
    (b) was struck with a rod by Moses
    (c) water flowed out quenching Israel's thirst

    Calvary's rock
    (a) was dead
    (b) was struck with a spear by a soldier
    (c) water flowed out quenching believer's thirst
4. The rock, having been previously struck, now needed only to be vocally addressed. Speaking to the rock in faith would cause the water to flow as it had many years earlier when the rock at Horeb was smitten.

5. The water from His side typified the Holy Spirit that Jesus provided by His crucifixion.
6. We drink the living water today by 'speaking to the rock' (Jesus) with words of love and adoration, and with a supernatural utterance (tongues) that the Spirit gives us.

If you have enjoyed this book and would like to help us to send a copy of it and many other titles to needy pastors in the **Third World**, please write for further information or send your gift to:

Sovereign World Trust
PO Box 777, Tonbridge
Kent TN11 9XT
United Kingdom

or to the **'Sovereign World'** distributor in your country.

If sending money from outside the United Kingdom, please send an International Money Order or Foreign Bank Draft in STERLING, drawn on a **UK** bank to **Sovereign World Trust**.